2003

Mom

Love,
Sandy

Catherine (Jones) Kraft

THREE YEARS

ON THE

PLAINS

THE DEATH OF JOHNSON IN COLORADO.

Frontispiece.

THREE YEARS
ON THE PLAINS

OBSERVATIONS OF INDIANS,
1867–1870

EDMUND B. TUTTLE

FOREWORD BY JEROME A. GREENE

UNIVERSITY OF OKLAHOMA PRESS
NORMAN

"Like an old pine-tree, I am dead at the top.
*   —Speech of an old chief*

Library of Congress Cataloging-in-Publication Data

Tuttle, Edmund B. (Edmund Bostwick), 1815–1881.
   [Boy's book about Indians]
   Three years on the Plains : observations of Indians,
1867–1870 / Edmund B. Tuttle ; foreword by Jerome A.
Greene—Red River books ed.
       p.   cm.—(The Western frontier library ; 66)
   Originally published: The boy's book about Indians.
London : Routledge, 1871.
   ISBN 0-8061-3499-2 (alk. paper)—ISBN 0-8061-3494-1
(pb. : alk. paper)
   1. Indians of North America. 2. Indians of North Ame-
ica—Great Plains. 3. Frontier and pioneer life—West (U.S.)
I. Title. II. Series.

E77.4 .T88 2002
978.004'97—dc21

                                        2002067526

The paper in this book meets the guidelines for permanence
and durability of the Committee on Production Guidelines for
Book Longevity of the Council on Library Resources, Inc.

First published as *The Boy's Book about Indians: Being What I
Saw and Heard for Three Years on the Plains* (London: Routledge, 1871; reprint, Philadelphia: J. P. Lippincott, 1873).

1 2 3 4 5 6 7 8 9 10

LETTER FROM GENERAL SHERMAN

HEADQUARTERS, ARMY OF THE UNITED STATES, WASHINGTON, D. C.,
June 13th, 1870.

Rev. E. B. TUTTLE, Fort D. A. Russell, W. T.

DEAR SIR,—I have your letter of June 8th, and do not, of
course, object to your dedicating your volume on Indians to
me. But please don't take your facts from the newspapers, that
make me out as favoring extermination.

I go as far as the farthest in favor of lavishing the kindness
of our people and the bounty of the general government on
those Indians who settle down to reservations and make the
least effort to acquire new habits; but to those who will not
settle down, who cling to their traditions and habits of hunting, of prowling along our long, thinly-settled frontiers, killing, scalping, mutilating, robbing, etc., the sooner they are
made to feel the inevitable result the better for them and
for us.

To those I would give what they ask, war, till they are
satisfied.

*   *   *   *   *   *   *   *

Yours truly,

W. T. SHERMAN, *General.*

CONTENTS

ILLUSTRATIONS

The Death of Johnson in Colorado *frontispiece*

MAP

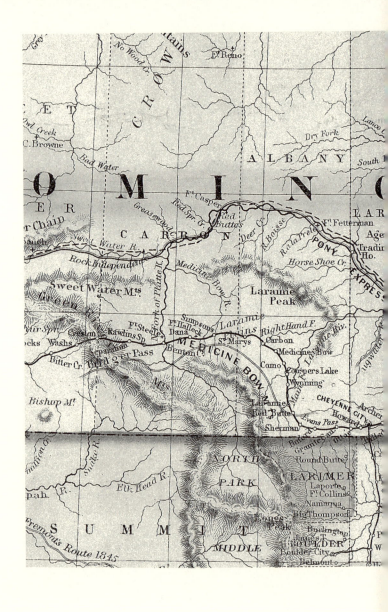

Detail from an 1877 map showing principal areas of Wyoming, Colorado, and Nebraska mentioned by Tuttle. Ft. D. A. Russell was located near Cheyenne, Wyoming. Original by S. Augustus Mitchell (1792–1868), 1" = 55 mi. Courtesy Jerome A. Greene.

FOREWORD

THE University of Oklahoma Press's republication of Edmund B. Tuttle's *Three Years on the Plains: Observations of Indians, 1867–1870* acknowledges a continuing interest among the public in the Indian wars of the trans-Mississippi West, including contemporary perspectives of those struggles. Tuttle's book initially appeared in the United States in 1872 (an 1871 London edition preceded), published by the well-known Philadelphia publisher J. B. Lippincott under the disarming title, *The Boy's Book about Indians: Being What I Saw and Heard for Three Years on the Plains*.[1] And while its content might have appealed to an 1870s juvenile audience, the little volume contained much that was timely about affairs on the Northern Plains affecting the nation's relations with several tribes, especially the Lakotas (or Teton Sioux), Northern Arapahos, and Northern Cheyennes. Appearing just six years after the establishment of army posts along the Bozeman Trail (from what is now north-central Wyoming—then part of Dakota Territory—to the Montana Territory gold fields) and the Fetterman military disaster near Fort Philip Kearny, it was one of but a few contemporary volumes that offered perspectives on the events by persons close to the scene.[2] As such, Tuttle's book provides readers something of immediacy from those days when prominent issues concerned matters of war and peace with American Indian tribes in the region.[3]

From its subject matter and presentation, the book might well be further subtitled *An Indian Miscellany*, for its content runs a curious gamut from the mythical origins of Indians (Tuttle—not surprisingly for the period—adheres to the Lost Tribes of Israel theory), to stories of their supposed savagery, to creation legends, and to existing naiveté about the Lakotas and other tribes. There are several factual errors that the author should have caught (e.g., Commissioner of Indian Affairs Ely S. Parker is referenced several times as a Chippewa [Ojibwa] Indian, when he was properly a Seneca; nor was the Southern Cheyenne leader, Black Kettle, killed at the Sand Creek Massacre in 1864—he died during Lieutenant Colonel George A. Custer's attack on his village at the Washita four years later), and Tuttle evinces occasional lapses in basic knowledge of Indians that he imparts in his text (e.g., confusing the Chippewas with the Tuscaroras as part of the Iroquois Confederacy). His reference to Red Cloud as being fifty-three in 1867 is wrong;

he was forty-five or forty-six years old at the time.[4]

Tuttle was U.S. Army chaplain at Fort D. A. Russell, near Cheyenne, Wyoming, when he prepared his manuscript. Although a man of the cloth, that position did not render him special enlightenment when it came to matters regarding American Indians, and his ideas consequently reflected an ignorance of, and subtle yet unmistakable denigration of, their lifeways that coincided with views commonly held among many whites of the time. Like many Americans, Tuttle did not distinguish traits of one tribe from those of another. He also believed that Indians, categorically, were "born and bred up among the wild beasts of the forest" and likely destined for extinction: "As good people come along, the Indian must *push on*, still farther toward the setting sun." "As a general thing," he wrote, "the Indian of our day is an untidy lord of the soil, over which he roams unfettered by any laws of society, and often—in his wild state—not controlled by its decencies or in possession of its privileges." Tuttle believed that this condition was largely "the fault of Christians more interested in foreign pagans, while neglecting these heathen at our own doors." Significantly, in a letter from William T. Sherman (included herein), to whom Tuttle dedicated his work, the Commanding General of the Army stated clearly that he did not advocate the extermination of the Indians, despite commonly held perceptions to the contrary of that officer's position on this inflammatory question. (It is, in effect, a "Sherman" statement on the matter of government-sponsored physical genocide.)

Despite errors grounded in ignorance and occasional inattentive generalities in describing American Indians and their conditions during the late 1860s and early 1870s, Tuttle presented in his book items of interest to later generations of readers and of particular value to historians. Included are accounts of towns like North Platte, Nebraska, and Greeley, Colorado Territory, and asides about hunting agates in the countryside around Fort Laramie, Wyoming. Importantly, Tuttle related several encounters with tribes in Wyoming, Colorado, and Nebraska that he had gleaned from correspondence or from other unspecified sources. Along with a contextual synopsis of Bozeman Trail events, including the annihilation of Captain William J. Fetterman's command (in which that officer is seen as a "noble, brave man" rather than the impetuous leader commonly perceived today), Tuttle related the fight between troops and Indians at Crazy Woman Fork of Powder River on July 20, 1866; an attack by Cheyennes on a stagecoach along the Platte River in Nebraska on June 1, 1867; a skirmish between Eighteenth infantrymen and Sioux near Fort Reno, Wyoming, in March 1868; a Sioux raid on Sidney

Station along the Union Pacific Railroad in the following month; and an engagement between troops of the Second Cavalry and Arapahos at Miner's Delight, Wyoming, on May 4, 1870.

Tuttle also described the government's negotiations with the Indians, efforts that in 1868 culminated in the army's abandonment of the posts along the Bozeman Trail and helped set the stage for sustained conflict with the tribes during the mid- to late 1870s. He gave particular attention to one council between peace commissioners and Sioux at Fort Phil Kearny on January 2, 1868, in which the Indians presented their assessment of events and reiterated their demands for closing the forts.[5] Tuttle further included a valuable contemporary description of the visit of a delegation of Lakotas with Chief Red Cloud to Washington, D.C., and New York City in June 1870. During meetings in the capital with government officials, including President Ulysses S. Grant, Red Cloud and other leaders unsuccessfully pressed for the removal of Fort Fetterman, which had been erected at the southern periphery of the disputed Powder River region in 1867, and vocally disavowed the boundaries established for the tribes in the Fort Laramie Treaty of 1868.[6]

Tuttle infused religious expressions into many of his remarks, doubtless to instill in young readers tenets of Christianity, a trait not surprising given his background as a clergyman. Yet little is

known of the man; his available military record
is brief, and his Appointment, Commission, and
Personnel file at the National Archives contains
but one document, an order of little consequence
that merely notes him along with several other
officers.[7] Nor did a search of the annual indexes
of the preeminent professional tabloid, *The Army
and Navy Journal*, disclose mention of either Tuttle or his book. We do know that Edmund Buterick
Tuttle was born in New York state in 1815, the
son of a physician.[8] He spent his youth in Auburn,
New York, where he first cultivated an interest
in Indians. At the outbreak of the Civil War, Tuttle was living in Illinois, working as a rector of a
Chicago parish. Between February 1861 and June
1862 he was acting post chaplain, and later post
chaplain, at Camp Douglas, Illinois. On June 20,
1862, he was appointed hospital chaplain with
the U.S. Volunteers, serving variously in that
capacity at Fort Donelson, Tennessee, and Mound
City, Illinois, until being mustered out on November 20, 1865. After the war, Tuttle joined the regulars as a captain, serving as post chaplain at
Fort Sedgwick, Colorado Territory, from September 1867 to February 1868, and thereafter at Fort
D. A. Russell. He died on April 30, 1881, at the age
of sixty-five or sixty-six. Tuttle's place of death
and its cause remain unknown.[9]

As an ordained clergyman, Tuttle was one of
but thirty post chaplains authorized in the army

(the four post–Civil War black regiments each had one, too). At Forts Sedgwick and D. A. Russell he ministered to the troops; his primary duties included conducting nondenominational religious services and performing burial rites for officers and soldiers. The chaplain further performed marriages and baptisms and made pastoral visits to those confined by sickness in the post hospital or undergoing punishment for offenses in the guard-house. By his demeanor and manner he often set the tone for the post, not only as spiritual advisor but as a teacher through sermons and lectures delivered to multi-faith congregations. He availed himself at all times for counsel and provided solace to soldiers and officers and their families whenever required. Beyond holding services, the chaplain's responsibilities often included leading Sunday school, song or choir practices, regular or occasional prayer meetings, and temperance meetings, and overseeing charity work. Too, Tuttle likely played a role in the operation of a post library, and perhaps taught enlisted men at a post school. As an educated and therefore presumably enlightened individual, his teaching skills extended beyond the pulpit and into the classroom.[10] Doubtless Tuttle's interest in Indian life and history manifested itself in the pursuit of his professional activities.

When *The Boy's Book about Indians* was published in 1872, *The Nation*'s reviewer critically forecasted that the content of "this disagreeable scrap-book" would, in fact, be frightful for American youth: "[It] is in no sense a boy's book; it treats of murders and horse-thieves as well as of Indians, is full of scenes of violence and slaughter, is wretchedly written and disorderly in the last degree, and, while it undoubtedly contains a great many true descriptions, it is calculated only to convince youthful readers that the Indians have thoroughly deserved their fate, whereas the author professes to aim at exciting sympathy on their behalf." Be that as it may, Tuttle's product today affords modern readers insight into the views of Indians held by many people during times of major conflict with them on the Plains. Because of the author's proximity to many of the events described, his book serves as a useful barometer of attitudes and perceptions of Americans in days long gone to history.

JEROME A. GREENE
April 2002

NOTES

1. The London version, of identical title, appeared under the publishing imprint of G. Routledge. Tuttle's other publications include *The History of Camp Douglas, Including Official Report of Gen. B. J. Sweet; with Anecdotes of the Rebel Prisoners* (Chicago: J. R. Walsh, 1865); *Six Months on the Plains: or, A Guide to Cheyenne and Rocky Mountains* (Chicago: Western News Co., 1868); and *Border Tales*

around the Camp Fire, in the Rocky Mountains (New York: E. P. Dutton; London: S. Low, Marston, Searle & Rivington, 1878).

2. The more widely known books were Margaret Irvin Carrington, *Ab-Sa-Ra-Ka, Home of the Crows: Being the Experience of an Officer's Wife on the Plains* (Philadelphia: J. P. Lippincott and Company, 1868); and George P. Belden, *Belden, the White Chief; or, Twelve Years Among the Wild Indians of the Plains* (Cincinnati and New York: C. F. Vent, 1870).

3. For background, see Robert M. Utley, *Frontier Regulars: The United States Army and the Indian, 1866–1890* (New York: Macmillan, 1973), 93–110. A thorough exposition of the events concerning the Fetterman affair is in Dee Brown, *Fort Phil Kearny: An American Saga* (New York: G. P. Putnam's Sons, 1962). For history of the Lakotas, see George E. Hyde, *Red Cloud's Folk: A History of the Oglala Sioux Indians* (Norman: University of Oklahoma Press, 1937); and George E. Hyde, *Spotted Tail's Folk: A History of the Brulé Sioux* (Norman: University of Oklahoma Press, 1961). For the Northern Cheyennes, see Peter J. Powell, *People of the Sacred Mountain: A History of the Northern Cheyenne Chiefs and Warrior Societies, 1830–1879, with an Epilogue, 1969–1974,* 2 vols. (San Francisco: Harper and Row, 1981); and George Bird Grinnell, *The Fighting Cheyennes* (Norman: University of Oklahoma Press, 1956). The Arapahos are treated in Virginia Cole Trenholm, *The Arapahoes: Our People* (Norman: University of Oklahoma Press, 1970). For the Bozeman Trail, including its military aspects, see Grace Raymond Hebard and Earl A. Brininstool, *The Bozeman Trail*, 2 vols. (Cleveland: The Arthur H. Clark Company, 1922; reprint, Glendale, Calif.: The Arthur H. Clark Company, 1960).

4. There is frequent mention of Red Cloud in the book. Modern treatments of this Lakota chief appear in Robert W. Larson, *Red Cloud: Warrior-Statesman of the Lakota Sioux* (Norman: University of Oklahoma Press, 1997); James C. Olson, *Red Cloud and the Sioux Problem* (Lincoln: University of Nebraska Press, 1965); and Hyde, *Red Cloud's Folk.*

5. Tuttle's presentation of the translation of the Lakotas' statements very closely follows that given in Belden, *The White Chief*, 389–93. For another account with several distinct differences from Tuttle/Belden, see Jerome A. Greene, ed., "'We do not know what the Government intends to do. . . .': Lt. Palmer Writes from the Bozeman Trail, 1867–68," *Montana The Magazine of Western History* 28 (July 1978), 27–29.

6. See also Larson, *Red Cloud*, 130–36; Olson, *Red Cloud and the Sioux Problem*, 96–113; and Hyde, *Red Cloud's Folk*, 173–81.

7. Edmund B. Tuttle ACP File N257 CB 1864, National Archives, Record Group 94, Records of the Office of the Adjutant General. This June 24, 1862, document is a notice of the commission of Tuttle and others as hospital chaplains.

8. Tuttle's middle name as "Buterick" appears in the authoritative Francis B. Heitman, comp., *Historical Register and Dictionary of the United States Army, from Its Organization, September 29, 1789, to March 2, 1903* (Washington, D.C.: Government Printing Office, 1903), 1:976. FirstSearch, OCLC's online catalog, lists both "Buterick" and "Bostwick."

9. Guy V. Henry, *Military Record of Civilian Appointments in the United States Army* (New York: Carleton, 1869), 478–79; Heitman, *Historical Register and Dictionary*, 1:976.

10. U.S. War Department, *Revised Regulations for the Army of the United States, 1861* (Philadelphia: J. B. Lippincott and Company, 1861), 36–37; George W. Simpson, *Manual for Post Chaplains* (n.p., 1893), 9–17; Don Rickey Jr., *Forty Miles a Day on Beans and Hay: The Enlisted Soldier Fighting the Indian Wars* (Norman: University of Oklahoma Press, 1963), 194–95. For a history of the U.S. Army chaplaincy during the late nineteenth and early twentieth centuries, see Earl Stover, *Up from Handyman: The U.S. Army Chaplaincy, 1865–1920* (Washington, D.C.: Department of the Army, 1977).

INTRODUCTION

THE interest which boys are taking in all that relates to our Indian tribes, and the greediness they manifest in devouring the sensational stories published so cheaply, filling their imaginations with stories of wild Indian life on the plains and borders, without regard to their truthfulness, cannot but be harmful; and therefore the writer, after three years' experience on the plains, feels desirous of giving youthful minds a right direction, in a true history of the red men of our forests. Thus can they teach their children, in time to come, what kind of races have peopled this continent; especially before civilization had marked them for destruction, and their hunting-grounds for our possession.

The RIGHTS and WRONGS of the Indians should be told fairly, in order that justice may be done to such as have befriended the white men who have met the Indians in pioneer life, and been befriended often by the savage, since the Mayflower landed her pilgrims on these shores some two hundred and fifty years ago.

The writer proposes now only a history of Indians since he began to know the "Six Nations" in Western New York, about forty years ago. Since then, these have dwindled down to a handful, and do not now exist in their separate tribal relations, but mixed in with others, far away from the beautiful lakes they once inhabited.

The origin of the native American Indian has puzzled the wisest heads.

The most plausible theory seems to be that they are one of the lost tribes of Israel; that they crossed a narrow frith from the confines of Asia, and that their traditions, it is said, go far to prove it.

For instance, the Sioux tell us that they were, many moons ago, set upon by a race larger in number than they, and were driven from the north in great fear, till they came to the banks of the North Platte, and finding the river swollen up to its banks, they were stopped there, with all their women, children, and horses. The enemy was pursuing, and their hearts grew white with fear. They made an offering to the Great Spirit, and he blew a wind into the water, so as to open a path on the bed of the river, and they all went

B   (13)

over in safety, and the waters, closing up, left their enemies on the other side. This, probably, is derived from a tradition of their forefathers, coming down to them from the passing of the children of Israel through the Red Sea.

Elias Boudinot, many years ago, and a minister in Vermont also, published books to show that the American Indians were a portion of the lost tribes, from resemblances between their religious customs and those of the Israelites. Later still, a converted Jew named Simon, undertook to identify the ancient South American races, Mexicans, Peruvians, etc., as descendants of ancient Israel, from similarity of language and of civil and religious customs. These authors have taken as their starting-point the resolution which, Esdras informs us (in the Apocrypha), the ten tribes took after being first placed in the cities of the Medes, viz., that they would leave the multitude of the heathen and go into a land wherein never mankind dwelt, that they might there keep their laws, which God gave them; and they suppose that, in pursuance of this resolution, the tribes continued in a northeasterly direction until they came to Behring Straits, which they crossed, and set foot on this continent, spreading over it from north to south, until, at the discovery of it by Columbus, they had peopled every part. It must be admitted that this theory is very plausible, and that if our Indians are not the descendants of the lost tribes of Israel, they show by their traditions and customs a knowledge of the ancient religion, such as calling the Great Spirit Yo-he-wah, the Jehovah of the Scriptures, and in many festivals corresponding to the Mosaic law.* The country to which the ten tribes, in a journey of a year and a half, would arrive, from the river Euphrates, east, would be somewhere adjoining Tartary, and intercourse between the two races would easily lead to the adoption of the religious ideas and customs of the one by the other.

The gypsy tribes came from Tartary, and in my intercourse with these wandering people, I found they had a custom somewhat like our Indians' practice, in removing from place to place. For instance, the gypsies, when they leave a part of their company to follow them, fix leaves in such wise as to direct their friends to follow in their course. This is called "*patteran*" in Romany or gypsy language. And the Indian cuts a notch in a tree as he passes through a forest, or places stones in the plains in such a way as to show in what direction he has gone. An officer saw a large stone, upon which an Indian had drawn the figure of a soldier on horseback, to indicate to others which way the soldiers had gone.

Origin of Evil.—They have a tradition handed down that the Great Spirit said they might eat

---

* Labagh.

of all the animals he had made, except the beaver. But some bad Indians went and killed a beaver, and the Great Spirit was angry and said they must all die. But after awhile he became willing that Indians should kill and eat them, so the beaver is hunted for his skin, and his meat is eaten as often as he suffers himself to be caught.

DESPOILING THE GRAVE OF AN OLD ONONDAGA CHIEF.

On-on-da-ga was the name of an Indian chief, who died about the year 1830, near Elbridge, a town lying north of Auburn, in the State of New York. This Indian belonged to the Onondagas, one of the tribes called " the Six Nations of the IROQUOIS" (E-ro-kwa), a confederacy consisting of the MOHAWKS, ONEIDAS, SENECAS, CAYUGAS, ONONDAGAS, and TUSCARORAS or CHIPPEWAS. I was a lad at the time of this chief's death, having my home in Auburn, New York, where my father was the physician and surgeon to the State prison. My father had a cousin, who was also a doctor and surgeon, a man of stalwart frame, raised in Vermont, named Cogswell. He was proud of his skill in surgery, and devoted to the science. He had learned of the death of the Onondaga chief, and conceived the idea of getting the body out of the grave for the purpose of dissecting the old fellow, —that is, of cutting him up and preserving his

bones to hang up on the walls of his office; of course, there was only one way of doing it, and that was by stealing the body under cover of night, as the Indians are very superstitious and careful about the graves of their dead. You know they place all the trappings of the dead— his bow and arrows, tomahawk and wampum —in the grave, as they think he will need them to hunt and supply his wants with on his journey to the happy hunting-grounds. They place food and tobacco, with other things, in the grave.

Dr. Cogswell took two men one night, with a wagon, and as the distance was only twelve miles, they performed the journey and got back safely before daylight, depositing the body of the Indian in a barn belonging to a Mr. Hopkins, in the north part of the town. It was soon noised about town what they had done, and there lived a man there who threatened to go and inform the tribe of the despoiling of the chief's grave, unless he was paid thirty dollars to keep silence. The doctor, being a bold, courageous man, refused to comply with a request he had no right to make, because it was an attempt to "levy black mail," as it is called.

Sure enough, he kept his word, and told the Onondagas, who were living between Elbridge and Syracuse. They were very much exasperated when they heard what had been done, and

B*   2

threatened vengeance on the town where the dead chief lay.

The tribe was soon called together, and a march was planned to go up to Auburn by the way of Skaneateles Lake,—a beautiful sheet of water lying six miles east of Auburn. They encamped in the pine woods,—a range called the "pine ridge,"—half-way between the two villages, and sent a few of the tribe into Auburn for the purpose of trading off the baskets they had made for powder and shot; but the real purpose they had in view was to find out just where the body was (deposited in the barn of Mr. Josiah Hopkins), intending to set fire to the barn and burn the town, rescuing the dead chief at the same time.

For several days the town was greatly excited, and every fireside at night was surrounded with anxious faces; the children listening with greedy ears to narratives of Indian cruelties perpetrated during the war with the English about Canada, in 1812; and I remember how it was told of a cruel Indian named Philip, that he would seize little babes from their mothers' arms and dash out their brains against the wall! No wonder we dreamed horrid dreams of the dusky faces every night.

At that time the military did not amount to much. There was a company of citizen soldiers there, called the " AUBURN GUARDS," numbering about forty men, with a captain whose name I forget, but who became suddenly seized with the idea of his unfitness to defend the town against the threatened Indian invasion, and did the wisest thing he could, and resigned his commission on a plea of "*sudden indisposition.*" The doctor walked the street as bold as a lion, but acting also with the shrewd cunning of the fox. And now, my young friends, instead of weaving a bloody romance in the style of the "Dime Novels," depicting the terrible massacre, which might have happened, with so great a wrong to provoke the hostility of the poor Indians, I am about to tell you how the town was saved, and how the doctor outwitted them. If you pause here, and guess, I think you will be far from the mark in reaching the shrewdness of the surgeon, who had not been bred among the hills of old Vermont for nothing.

As I said, at Auburn there is a State prison, and when the convicts die, their bodies, unless claimed by relatives or friends within twenty-four hours after death, are at the disposal of the surgeon for dissection.

As good luck would have it, a negro convict died at the time of our story; and the doctor conceived the idea of getting out of his difficulty by transferring the dead body of the negro Jim to the despoiled empty grave of Onondaga! This done, he easily persuaded the Indians to go back and find the body of their chief all right: and so he succeeded in humbugging the weak-minded Indians, while the bones of old Onondaga were duly prepared and hung up to show students how Indians and all men are made of bone and muscle. The doctor thought he had done a good thing; but when I went into the office and saw the horrid skull grinning at me, I was thankful that the spirit of old Onondaga could not say of me, "You did it!"

II.

The most notable of the chiefs belonging to the Six Nations were Hiawatha, Thayendanega (or Brant, his English name), Sagoyewatha, or Red Jacket,—the most intelligent of the chiefs, and who is said to have been the uncle of General Parker, a full-blood Chippewa, and at one time Indian Commissioner at Washington. (Parker served as an aide of General Grant during the war. In early life, he was a pupil at the normal school, in Albany; and was reckoned quite a proficient in music by Prof. Bowen.)

Most of these tribes, inhabiting the country bordering on the Mohawk River, Onondaga Lake, Skaneateles, Owasco, Cayuga, Seneca, Ontario, and Erie, migrated at an early day to Green Bay, and to the Straits of Mackinaw. As remnants of the Onondagas were passing through Auburn, they often slept on the floor of our kitchen, and they never stole anything or did us any harm. One day, they were passing the American Hotel, and, as usual, begged a few sixpences of all they met. A gentleman sitting on the porch said to one of them, " No, you'll spend it for whisky."

" Oh, no," he replied; "*give it to my wife,—he's a Methodist woman!*"

I met a tribe of Chippewas at Marquette, a short time since, on Lake Superior, whither they had migrated from Green Bay. *An-ges-ta*, the chief, was a tall, noble-looking fellow. He wanted the church to help his people, who were very poor.

Said he, " We lived in Green Bay a great while, but when I looked into our cabins and saw so many of them empty, and into the grave-yard, and counted more graves than we had living, my heart was sad, and I went away farther toward the setting sun !"

He made an eloquent speech to the Prince of Wales on his visit to the West, and it was pronounced a fine piece of natural oratory.

A few remnants of the New York tribes are living not far from Buffalo, on a reservation, where they cultivate farms and have schools and churches.

Such were the Oneidas, Onondagas, Cayugas, Senecas, Mohawks, and Chippewas. Only one band is left in New York State now, that of the Onondagas.

The present generation of grown people have read with delight the beautiful novels of J. Fenimore Cooper, Esq., but they have been disappointed in not finding any living examples of his noble heroes. As a general thing, the Indian of our day is an untidy lord of the soil, over which he roams unfettered by any laws of society, and often—in his wild state—not controlled by its decencies or in possession of its privileges. But I think this is the fault of Christians more interested in foreign pagans, while neglecting these heathen at our own doors.

THE FIDELITY OF AN INDIAN CHIEF.

The following story about an Oneida chief is told by Judge W——:

Early in the settlement of the western part of New York, the judge was living in Whitesboro', four miles west of Utica. All around was an unbroken forest of beech, maple, and other trees, held by wild tribes of Indians, who had been for ever so long owners of the soil. Judge W——, feeling how much he was at their mercy in his lonely place, was anxious to keep on good terms with them, and secure their friendship in return.

Many of the chiefs had heard of his friendly ways, and went to see him, carrying presents, because of the gifts he had sent them; but he was much troubled that an old chief of the tribe, having great influence with his people, had never come to see him, or sent him any presents, or shown any signs of welcome. After awhile the judge made up his mind to go and see the sachem in his wigwam, and thus secure a friendship he might rely on in case of any difficulty. His family was small,—only his daughter, a widow, and her only child, a fine boy, five years old. So, one day he went to pay the chief a visit, taking the widow and her son along with him. He found him seated at the door of his tent, enjoying a nice breeze of a fine summer's morning, and was welcomed by the old chief with kind manners and the word "Sago," meaning, "How do you do?" Judge W—— presented his daughter and her little boy to the old chief, and said they had come to live in his country; they were anxious to live in peace with them, and introduce among them the arts of civilization. Listening to these words, the chief said,—

"Brother, you ask much and promise much; what pledge can you give of your good faith?"

Judge.—" The honor of a man who never knew deceit."

Sachem.—"The white man's word may be good to the white man, yet it is but wind when spoken to the Indian."

Judge.—" I have put my life into your hands by coming hither; is not this a proof of my good intentions? I have trusted the Indian, and I will not believe that he will abuse or betray my trust."

"So much is well," said the chief; "the Indian repays trust with trust: if you will hurt him, he will hurt you. But I must have a pledge. Leave this boy with me in my wigwam, and I will bring him back to you in three days with my answer."

If an arrow had pierced the bosom of the young mother, she could not have felt a sharper pang than that which the Indian's proposal had caused her.

She flew towards her boy, who stood beside the chief looking into his face with pleased and innocent wonder, and, snatching him to her arms, would have rushed away with him.

A gloomy frown came over the sachem's brow, and he remained silent.

The judge knew that all their lives depended upon a right action at once; and following his daughter, who was retreating with her child into the woods, he said to her, " Stay, stay, my daughter; bring back the child, I beg of you ! I would not risk a hair of his head, for he is as dear to me as to you,—but, my child, he must remain with the chief! God will watch over him, and he will be as safe in the sachem's wigwam as in your arms beneath your own roof." She yielded, and her darling boy was left; but who can tell the agony of the mother's heart during the following days?

Every night she awoke from her sleep, seeming to hear the screams of her child calling upon its mother for help. How slowly and heavily passed the hours away. But at last the third day came. The morning waned away, and the afternoon was far advanced, yet the chief came not. There was sorrow over the whole home, and the mother, pale and silent, walked her room in despair. The judge, filled with anxious doubts and fears, looked through the opening in the forest towards the sachem's abode.

At last, as the rays of the setting sun were thrown upon the tops of the tall trees around, the eagle feathers of the chief were seen dancing above the bushes in the distance. He came rapidly, and the little boy was at his side. He was gayly attired as a young chief: his feet dressed in moccasins, a fine beaver-skin thrown over his shoulders, and eagle's feathers stuck in his hair. He was laughing and gay, and so proud of his honors that he seemed two inches taller than before. He was soon clasped in his mother's arms, and in that brief moment of joy she seemed to pass from death to life.

"The white man has conquered!" said the chief; "hereafter let us be friends. You have trusted the Indian; he will repay you with confidence and kindness."

And he was true to his word. Judge W——— lived many years, laying there the foundation of

c

that flourishing community which has spread over a wide extent of western New York.

The Far West, in my childhood, meant the " Genesee country," as far as the falls of Niagara.

BIG THUNDER—A WINNEBAGO CHIEF.

The Winnebago Indians migrated from Belvidere, Illinois, on the Kish-wau-kie River, to Minnesota, and thence to the Omaha reservation, in Nebraska. At Belvidere, there is a mound on which Big Thunder when he died was set up, his body supported by posts driven in the ground. This was done at his dying request, and in accord with his prophecy to his tribe: " That there was to be a great and terrible fight between the white and red men. And when the red men were about to be beaten in the battle, he would come to life again, and rising up with a shout, would lead his people to victory!" His tribe would visit the spot once a year, where his body was drying away, and leave tobacco as an offering; and the white young men would surely go there soon after and stow the plugs away in their capacious pockets. As the town became settled, visitors would carry off the bones as mementos of the old chief. After they were all gone, some wags would place the bones of some dead sheep for relic-hunters to pick up and carry home as the bones of a noble chief.

I have seen the stakes, which was all that re-

mained of " Big Thunder" after he was dried up
and blown away.

INDIAN TRADITION—THE DELUGE.

The Oneidas have a tradition about the deluge,
which is very singular. According to their story,
an unlimited expanse of water covered the whole
space now occupied by the world we live in.

At this time the whole human family dwelt in
a country situated in the upper regions of the
air. Everything needed for comfort and pleasure
was found. The people did not know what death
was, nor its attendant, sickness or disease ; and
their minds were free from jealousy, hatred, or
revenge.

At length it happened that all of this was
changed, and care and trouble came to them.

A certain youth was seen to withdraw himself
from the circle of social amusements, and he
wandered away alone in the groves, as his favorite resort.

Care and sorrow marked his countenance, and
his body, from long abstinence from food, began
to make him look to his friends like a skeleton
of a man. Anxious looks could not solve the
mystery of his grief; and by-and-by, weakened
in body and soul, he yielded to his companions, and promised to disclose the cause of his
trouble, on condition that they would dig up

by the roots a certain pine-tree, lay him in his blanket by the edge of the hole, and place his wife by his side; at once all hands were ready. The fatal tree was taken up by the roots; in doing which the earth was opened, and a passage made into the abyss below. The blanket was spread by the hole; the youth lay upon it the wife also (soon to be a mother) took her seat by his side. The crowd, anxious to know the cause of such strange and unheard-of conduct, pressed close around; when, all of a sudden, to their horror and surprise, he seized upon the woman and threw her headlong into the regions of darkness below! Then, rising from the ground, he told the people that he had for some time suspected that his wife was untrue to him, and so, having got rid of the cause of his trouble, he would soon recover his health and spirits.

All those amphibious animals which now inhabit this world then roamed through the watery waste to which this woman, in her fall, was now hastening. The loon first discovered her coming, and called a council in haste to prepare for her reception,—observing that the animal which approached was a human being, and that earth was necessary for its accommodation. The first thing to be thought of was, who should support the burden?

The sea-bear first presented himself for a trial of his strength. At once the other animals gathered round and jumped upon his back; while the bear, unable to bear up such a weight, sank beneath the water, and was by all the crowd judged unequal to support the weight of the earth. Several others presented themselves, were tried, and found wanting. But last of all came the turtle, modestly tendering his broad shell as the basis of the earth now to be formed. The beasts then made a trial of his strength to bear by heaping themselves on his back, and finding by their united pressure they could not sink him below the surface, adjudged him the honor of supporting the world on his back.

Thus, a foundation being found, the next subject of thought was how to procure earth. Several of the most expert divers plunged to the bottom of the sea and came up dead; but the *mink* at last though he shared the same fate, brought up in his claws a small quantity of dirt. This was placed on the back of the turtle.

In the mean while the woman kept on falling, till at last she alighted on the turtle's back. The earth had already grown to the size of a man's foot where she stood, with one foot covering the other. By-and-by she had room for both feet, and was able to sit down. The earth continued to expand, and when its plain was covered with green grass, and streams ran, which poured into the ocean, she built her a house on the sea-shore. Not long after, she had a daughter, and she lived

c*

on what grew naturally, till the child was grown to be a woman. Several of the animals wanted to marry her, they being changed into the forms of young men; but the mother would not consent, until the turtle offered himself as a beau, and was accepted. After she had lain herself down to sleep, the turtle placed two arrows on her body, in the shape of a cross : one headed with flint, the other with the rough bark of a tree. By-and-by she had two sons, but died herself.

The grandmother was so angry at her death that she threw the children into the sea. Scarcely had she reached her wigwam when the children had overtaken her at the door. She then thought best to let them live; and dividing the body of her daughter in two parts, she threw them up toward the heavens, when one became the sun, the other the moon. Then day and night first began. The children soon grew up to be men, and expert with bow and arrows. The elder had the arrow of the turtle, which was pointed with flint; the younger had the arrow pointed with bark. The first was, by his temper and skill and success in hunting, a favorite of his grandmother. They lived in the midst of plenty, but would not allow the younger brother, whose arrow was insuffi-cient to kill anything but birds, to share with their abundance.

As this young man was wandering one day along the shore, he saw a bird perched on a limb hanging over the water. He aimed to kill it, but his arrow, till this time always sure, went aside the mark, and sank into the sea.

He determined to recover it, and made a dive for the bottom. Here, to his surprise, he found himself in a small cottage. A fine-looking old man sitting there welcomed him with a smile, and thus spoke to him : " My son, I welcome you to the home of your father ! To obtain this meeting I directed all the circumstances which have combined to bring you hither. Here is your arrow, and an ear of corn. I have watched the unkindness of your brother, and now command you to take his life. When you return home, gather all the flints you can find, and hang up all the deer's horns. These are the only things which will make an impression on his body, which is made of flint."

Having received these instructions, the young Indian took his leave, and, in a quarrel with his brother, drove him to distant regions, far beyond the savannas, in the southwest, where he killed him, and left his huge flint form in the earth. (Hence the Rocky Mountains.) The great enemy to the race of the turtle being thus destroyed, they sprang from the ground in human form, and multiplied in peace.

The grandmother, roused to furious resentment at the loss of her favorite son, resolved to be revenged.

For many days she caused the rain to descend from the clouds in torrents, until the whole surface of the earth, and even the highest mountains, were covered. The inhabitants escaped by fleeing to their canoes. She then covered the earth with snow ; but they betook themselves to their snow-shoes. She then gave up the hope of destroying them all at once, and has ever since employed herself in inflicting smaller evils on the world, while her younger son displays his good and benevolent feelings by showering blessings on his race.

[For this tradition I am indebted to N. P. Willis, Esq., whose visits to my house in New York were among the events of early days never to be forgotten.]

TRIBES ON THE PLAINS.

The Indian tribes on the plains, altogether, with those of New Mexico, Texas, California, and Arizona, do not exceed 300,000, including Indians, squaws, and papooses. They are as follows:

Dakota.—Sioux (pronounced Soos), of these there are several bands, under chiefs for each band, called Yanktons, Poncas, Lower Brules, Lower Yanctonais, Two Kettle Sioux, Blackfeet, Minneconjons, Uncpapas, Ogallahs, Upper Yanctonais, Sansarc, Wahpeton Sioux, Arickarees, Gros Ventres, Mandans, Assinaboins, Sipetons, Santee.

Hah-tah-pah, Black Horn.
Zin-tak-gah-lat-skah, Spotted Tail.
Zin-tah-skah, White Tail.
Me-wah-tak-ne-ho-skah, Tall Mandas.
He-cha-chat-kah, Bad Left Hand.
No-mah-no-pah, Two and Two.

Spotted Tail, who was at Fort D. A. Russell
in 1868, just after the treaty, wore a coon-skin
cap,—hence called Spotted Tail. Each chief gets
his peculiar name from some event in his life, or
some peculiarity of person, as for instance,—

Tah-shun-ka-co-qui-pah, Man-afraid-of-his-
horses. His horse stampeded one day, when his
tribe was fighting some other one, and ran into
the ranks of the enemy. When his owner got
back again, he left his horse behind and *went in*
(as we say), on foot, to fight again. It is not a
term of reproach, as he was not a coward, but
did not want to lose his horse,—hence called
" Man-afraid-of-his-horses."

Ogallahs.

Tah-shun-ka-co-qui-pah, his x mark, Man
afraid-of-his-horses.
Sha-ton-skah, his x mark, White Hawk.
Sha-ton-sapah, his x mark, Black Hawk.
E-ga-mon-ton-ka-sapah, his x mark, Black
Tiger.

Oh-wah-she-cha, his x mark, Bad Wound.

Pah-gee, his x mark, Grass.

Wah-non-reh-che-geh, his x mark, Ghost Heart.

Con-reeh, his x mark, Crow.

Oh-he-te-kah, his x mark, The Brave.

Tah-ton-kah-he-yo-ta-kah, his x mark, Sitting Bull.

Shon-ka-oh-wah-mon-ye, his x mark, Whirl-wind Dog.

Ha-hah-kah-tah-miech, his x mark, Poor Elk.

Wam-bu-lee-wah-kon, his x mark, Medicine Eagle.

Chon-gah-ma-he-to-hans-ka, his x mark, High Wolf.

Wah-se-chun-ta-shun-kah, his x mark, Ameri-can Horse.

Mah-hah-mah-ha-mak-near, his x mark, Man that walks under the ground.

Mah-to-tow-pah, his x mark, Four Bears.

Ma-to-wee-sha-kta, his x mark, One that kills the bear.

Oh-tah-kee-toka-wee-chakta, his x mark, One that kills in a hard place.

Tah-tonka-skah, his x mark, White Bull.

Con-ra-washta, his x mark, Pretty Coon.

Ha-cah-cah-she-chah, his x mark, Bad Elk.

Wa-ha-ka-zah-ish-tah, his x mark, Eye Lance.

Ma-to-ha-ke-tah, his x mark, Bear that looks behind.

Bella-tonka-tonka, his x mark, Big Partisan.

Mah-to-ho-honka, his x mark, Swift Bear.

To-wis-ne, his x mark, Cold Place.

Ish-tah-skah, his x mark, White Eyes.

Ma-ta-loo-zah, his x mark, Fast Bear.

As-hah-kah-nah-zhe, his x mark, Standing Elk.

Can-te-te-ki-ya, his x mark, The Brave Heart.

Shunka-shaton, his x mark, Day Hawk.

Tatanka-wakon, his x mark, Sacred Bull.

Mapia-shaton, his x mark, Hawk Cloud.

Ma-sha-a-ow, his x mark, Stands and Comes.

Shon-ka-ton-ka, his x mark, Big Dog.

Tah-ton-kak-ta-miech, The Poor Bull.

Oh-huns-ee-ga-non-sken, Mad Shade.

Thah-ton-oh-na-an-minne-ne-oh-minne, Whirl-ing Hand.

Mah-to-chun-ka-oh, Bear's Back.

Che-ton-wee-koh, Fool Hawk.

Wah-ho-ke-zah-ah-hah, One that has the Lance.

Shon-gah-manni-toh-tan-kak-seh, Big Wolf Foot.

Eh-ton-kah, Big Mouth.

(This was the first Indian I saw at North Platte, when we came there in 1867. Looking out of the car window, I called my wife's attention to a big Indian, and said, " Did you ever see such a big mouth before ?" Sure enough, it was the chief, and he was killed in a drunken row in Dakota recently, having been shot by Spotted Tail.)

Ma-pa-che-tah, Bad Hand.

Wah-ke-gun-shah, Red Thunder.

D

Wak-sah, One that cuts off.
Cham-nom-qui-yah, One that presents the Pipe.
Wah-ke-ke-yan-puh-tah, Fire Thunder.
Mah-to-neuk-pah-ze, Bear with Yellow Ears.
Con-reh-teh-kah, The Little Crow.
He-hup-pah-toh, The Blue War Club.
Shon-kee-toh, The Blue Horse.
Wam-balla-oh-conguo, Quick Eagle.
Ta-tonka-juppah, Black Bull.
Mo-to-ha-she-na, The Bear Hide.

Yanctonais.

Mah-to-non-pah, his x mark, Two Bears.
Mah-to-hua-skin-ya, his x mark, Mad Bear.
He-o-pu-za, his x mark, Lousy.
Ah-ke-che-tah-che-ca-dan, his x mark, Little
Soldier.
Mah-to-e-tan-chan, his x mark, Chief Bear.
Cu-wi-h-win, his x mark, Rotten Stomach.
Skun-ka-we-tko, his x mark, Fool Dog.
Ish-ta-sap-pah, his x mark, Black Eye.
Ih-tan-chan, his x mark, the Chief.
I-a-wi-ca-ka, his x mark, The One who tells
the Truth.
Ah-ke-che-tah, his x mark, The Soldier.
Ta-shi-na-gi, his x mark, Yellow Robe.
Nah-pe-ton-ka, his x mark, Big Hand.
Chan-tee-we-kto, his x mark, Fool Heart.
Hog-gau-sah-pa, his x mark, Black Catfish.

Mah-to-wah-kan, his x mark, Medicine Bear.

Shun-ka-kan-sha, his x mark, Red Horse.

Wan-rode, his x mark, The Eagle.

Can-hpi-sa-pa, his x mark, Black Tomahawk.

War-he-le-re, his x mark, Yellow Eagle.

Cha-ton-che-ca, his x mark, Small Hawk, or Long Fare.

Shu-ger-mon-e-too-ha-ska, his x mark, Tall Wolf.

Ma-to-u-tah-kah, his x mark, Sitting Bear.

Hi-ha-cah-ge-na-skene, his x mark, Mad Elk.

Arapahoes.

Little Chief, his x mark.

Tall Bear, his x mark.

Top Man, his x mark.

Neva, his x mark.

The Wounded Bear, his x mark.

Whirlwind, his x mark.

The Fox, his x mark.

The Dog Big Mouth, his x mark.

Spotted Wolf, his x mark.

Minneconjons.

Heh-non-ge-chat, One Horn.

Oh-pon-ah-tah-e-manne, The Elk that bellows Walking.

Heb-ho-lah-reh-cha-skah, Young White Bull.

Wah-cha-chum-kah-coh-kee-pah, One that is afraid of Shield.

He-hon-ne-shakta, The Old Owl.

Moe-pe-a-toh, Blue Cloud.

Oh-pong-ge-le-skah, Spotted Elk.

Tah-tonk-ka-hon-ke-schne, Slow Bull.

Shunk - a - nee - skah - skah-a-tah-pe, The Dog Chief.

Mah-to-tab tonk-kah, Bull Bear.

Wom-beh-le-ton-kah, The Big Eagle.

Ma-to-eh-schne-lah, his x mark, the Lone Bear.

Mah-toh-ke-su-yah, his x mark, The One who remembers the Bear.

Ma-toh-oh-he-to-keh, his x mark, the Brave Bear.

Eh-che-ma-heh, his x mark, The Runner.

Ti-ki-ya, his x mark, The Hard.

He-ma-za, his x mark, Iron Horn.

Sorrel Horse.

Black Coal.

Big Wolf.

Knock-Knee.

Black Crow.

The Lone Old Man.

Paul.

Black Bull.

Big Track.

Black White.

Yellow Hair.

Little Shield.

Black Bear.

Wolf Moccasin.

Big Robe.
Wolf Chief.
Friday.
The Foot.
And lastly, "Stinking Saddle-Cloth!"

Uncpapa Sioux.

Co-kam-i-ya-ya, his x mark, The Man that goes in the Middle.

Ma-to-ca-wa-weksa, his x mark, Bear Rib.

Ta - to - ka - in - yan - ke, his x mark, Running Antelope.

Kan-gi-wa-ki-ta, his x mark, Looking Crow.

A-ki-ci-ta-han-ska, his x mark, Long Soldier.

Wa-ku-te-ma-ni, his x mark, The One who shoots Walking.

Un-kca-ki-ka, his x mark, The Magpie.

Kan-gi-o-ta, his x mark, Plenty Crow.

He-ma-za, his x mark, Iron Horn.

Shun-ka-i-na-pin, his x mark, Wolf Necklace.

I-we-hi-yu, his x mark, The Man who Bleeds from the Mouth.

He-ha-ka-pa, his x mark, Elk Head.

I-zu-za, his x mark, Grind Stone.

Shun ka-wi-tko, his x mark, Fool Dog.

Ma-kpi-ya-po, his x mark, Blue Cloud.

Wa-mln-pi-lu-ta, his x mark, Red Eagle.

Ma-to-can-te, his x mark, Bear's Heart.

A-ki-ci-ta-i-tau-can, his x mark, Chief Soldier.

D*

Blackfeet Sioux.

Can-te-pe-ta, his x mark, Fire Heart.

Wan-mdi-kte, his x mark, The One who kills Eagle.

Sho-ta, his x mark, Smoke.

Wan-mdi-ma-ni, his x mark, Walking Eagle.

Wa-shi-cun-ya-ta-pi, his x mark, Chief White Man.

Kan-gi-i-yo-tan-ke, his x mark, Sitting Crow.

Pe-ji, his x mark, The Grass.

Kda-ma-ni, his x mark, The One that rattles as he Walks.

Wah-han-ka-sa-pa, his x mark, Black Shield.

Can-te-non-pa, his x mark, Two Hearts.

Ogallalla Sioux.

To-ka-in-yan-ka, his x mark, The One who goes ahead Running.

Ta-tan-ka-wa-kin-yan, his x mark, Thunder Bull.

Sin-to-min-sa-pa, his x mark, All over Black.

Can-i-ca, his x mark, The One who took the Stick.

Pa-tan-ka, his x mark, Big Head.

Two-Kettle Band.

Ma-wa-tan-ni-han-ska, his x mark, Long Mandan.

Can-kpe-du-ta, his x mark, Red War Club.

Can-ka-ga, his x mark, The Log.

Sansareh Sioux.

He-na-pin-wa-ni-ca, his x mark, The One that has neither Horn.

Wa-inlu-pi-lu-ta, his x mark, Red Plume.

Ci-tan-gi, his x mark, Yellow Hawk.

He-na-pin-wa-ni-ca, his x mark, No Horn.

Santee Sioux.

Wa-pah-shaw, his x mark, Red Ensign.

Wah-koo-tay, his x mark, Shooter.

Hoo-sha-sha, his x mark, Red Legs.

O-wan-cha-du-ta, his x mark, Scarlet all over.

Wau-mace-tan-ka, his x mark, Big Eagle.

Cho-tan-ka-e-na-pe, his x mark, Flute-player.

Ta-shun-ke-mo-za, his x mark, His Iron Dog.

In Washington Territory are five bands, such as the
Spokans, Pend d'Oreilles, etc., in all...................... 9,285
California.—Seven bands, such as Wylackies, etc....... 25,225
Arizona.—Apaches, Yumas, Mohaves, etc................. 31,570
Oregon.—Walla-Wallas, Cayuses, etc...................... 10,942
Utah.—Utahs and Utes... 25,250
Nevada.—Pi-utes, Shoshones, Bannacks, Washoes, etc. 8,200
New Mexico.—Navajoes, Pueblos, Jicarilla Apaches,
etc. (with 2000 captives held in peonage,—*i.e.*
slavery) 20,036
Colorado.—U-in-tak, Utes.................................... 5,000
Dakota, including Wyoming, set off from Dakota:
Yancton Sioux.. 2,500
Poncas... 979
Lower Brules... 1,600
Lower Yanctonais... 2,250

44

Two-Kettle Sioux	750
Blackfeet	1,200
Minneconjons	3,060
Uncpapas	3,000
Ogallallas	3,000
Upper Yanctonais	2,400
Sansarc	720
Wahpeton Sioux	1,637
Arickarees	1,500
Gros Ventres	400
Mandans	400
Assinaboins	2,640
Sissetons and other Sioux	3,500
	31,534

Montana.—Piegans, Blackfeet, Flatheads, Gros Ventres, Kootenays, Crôws, etc. ... 19,560

Nebraska and Kansas.—Winnebagoes, Omahas, Pawnees, Sacs and Foxes of Missouri, Iowas, Cheyennes, Arapahoes, and Santee Sioux ... 17,995

Central Agency, in Kansas and Indian Territory.—Pottawatamies, Shawnees, Delaware, Osages, Senecas, Kaws, Kickapoos, Ottawas, Comanches, Arapahoes, Cheyennes, and Apaches ... 17,422

Southern Agency, Cherokee Country.—Creeks, Cherokees, Choctaws, Chickasaws, Seminoles, Wichitas, Keechies, Wolves, Tuscaroras, Caddoes, Shawnees, Delawares, etc. ... 48,145

Green Bay Agency.—Oneidas, Menominees, and Munsees ... 3,036

Wisconsin.—Chippeways of Mississippi ... 6,179

Lake Superior.—Chippewas, etc., wandering ... 6,114

Mackinac.—Pottawatamies, etc. ... 8,099

New York State.—Cattaraugas, Cayugas, Onondagas, with Senecas, Allegany, Tonawandas, Tuscaroras, Oneidas, Onondagas ... 4,136

Total ... 298,528

FRIDAY was found on the Plains many years ago, while a lad, by Father de Smet, a Jesuit missionary, and taken to St. Louis, where he was educated. He returned again to his tribe, and leads a roving life. In November, 1869, he came to our post with Medicine-Man, Little Wolf, Sorrel Horse, and Cut-Foot, having been brought down by General Augur, Commander of the Department of the Platte, to go up the Union Pacific Railroad, as far as Wind River Valley, to meet old Waskakie, head chief of the Shoshones, and to make a treaty with his tribe, fearing the southern Sioux and Cheyennes would make war upon Friday's band, which numbered only fifteen hundred. Not finding Waskakie on his reservation, they waited several weeks for his return from the mountains, where he was gone on a hunt for his winter's supply of buffalo and deer meat. After waiting as long as they could, the Arapahoes left some of their arrows for Waskakie, that he might know they had been there, and also brought back some of the Shoshones' arrows, to convince the Arapahoe Indians that they had fulfilled their mission.

At this time, Friday had a beautiful set of arrows, bow and quiver, which I desired to purchase and carry east, to show Sunday-school children the weapons of Indian warfare, and how they kill their game. Friday would not sell his "outfit," as it is called, for money, but was willing to "trade" for a revolver, with which he said he could hunt buffalo. At first, the Indian agent said it was unlawful to sell firearms and ammunition to the Indians. This I told Friday. He then said, " *Well, let's trade on the sly.*" This I declined to do. But after a few days, I got permission, and took Friday into Cheyenne, to select the pistol. After picking out a good one, he then begged for bullet-mould, lead, powder, and caps. A trade is never complete with an Indian as long as he sees anything he can get added to the bargain.

General Duncan, of the 5th Cavalry, tells me of one of his trades with a red man at Fort Laramie. His little boy took a fancy to an Indian pony one day, and the general offered to exchange a nice *mule* for the pony. This was soon done and settled, as the general supposed. But next day the Indian came back and demanded some tobacco, sugar, flour, etc. "What for?" demanded the general. The Indian gave him to understand that he did trade horses, but as the mule had little or no tail, and the pony a long one, " *he wanted the sugar, tobacco, and flour to make up for the tail!*" After Friday and his fellow-chiefs had left us, some one wrote this to a Chicago paper, as follows :

THE AUTHOR A MEDICINE-MAN.

The Indians sometimes confer "brevets" on distinguished individuals as marks of favor, though they do not, or have not as yet, scattered them in like profusion, as in the army, so that the whole thing has become a farce.

Mr. Catlin, or Mr. Schoolcraft (Indian writers and painters), was made a regular chief of the Chippewas in the time of Red Jacket, a big chief at Tonawanda. In the month of November, 1869, five Arapahoe chiefs came to Fort Russell,— "Friday," "Little Wolf," "Cut-Foot," "Sorrel Horse," and "Head Medicine-Man." On account of many little kindnesses to them while remaining, Friday invited the writer to go up with the party to their home among the Black Hills, where he could be initiated into the forms of a civil chief. Friday said, "These fellows" —meaning his companions—"think a big heap of you, and want you to go home with them." As the ceremony includes a dog feast, it was postponed for awhile. They called me "The White Medicine-Man,"—and the feast has been partaken of at different times by some officers on the plains, who say dog's meat tastes much like mutton. A feast was made, it is said, at Fort Laramie for the Peace Commission, which met there in 1868. There were Generals Sherman, Harney, Augur, Terry, Sanborn, and Col. Tap-

48

pan present. A big chief had given the entertainment of dog, in soup, roast, etc. Having only
one big tin dish to serve the soup in, and it being
rather dirty, the old squaw seized a pup to wipe
it out with. But the old chief felt mortified at
it, and so he tore off a piece of his shirt and gave
the pan an extra wipe !

THE SIOUX SUN DANCE—SCENE ON THE PLAINS OF
YOUNG WARRIORS EXHIBITING FORTITUDE AND
RRAVERY IN TORTURING PAINS—A HORRIBLE
SCENE.

Red Cloud, a head chief, lives in what is called
the Powder River country, above Fort Fetterman. But the Sioux nation roam for hundreds
of miles all over the plains, and are sure to turn
up just when and where they are least expected.

These Sioux, the most numerous of all the
Indian tribes, have a festive performance, which
is regarded by all civilized people with horror
and abhorrence, and one which few can look
upon with nerve enough to see the end.

It is a sort of religious dance, in which the
young braves test their fortitude and stoicism in
resisting pain and torture without wincing. A
young officer, who witnessed the " Sun Dance"
last year, at the Cheyenne agency, a few miles
above Fort Sully, on the Missouri River, gives
the following account:

" The Indians manifested considerable opposition to having any whites present. When several officers belonging to the 17th United States Infantry came up, Red Leaf—a chief of Red Cloud's band—leaped over a breastwork of logs and ordered the troops away. After parleying with the chief some time, the soldiers fell back and took a position which was not objectionable to the Indians, but from which they could obtain only a partial view of the performances. There was a large lodge, built in shape of an amphitheatre, with a hole in the centre. The sides and roof were covered with willows, forming a tolerable screen, but not so dense as to obstruct entirely the view. The performances began with low chants and incantations. Five young men were brought in and partially stripped, their mothers being present and assisting in the ceremony.

"Then the 'Medicine-man' began his part by cutting slits in the flesh of the young men and taking up the muscles with pincers. The old squaws assisted in lacerating the flesh of the boys with sharp knives. The squaws would at the same time keep up a howling, accompanied with a backward-and-forward movement. When the muscles were lifted out by pincers on the breast, one end of a kind of lariat (used for fastening horses while grazing), or buffalo thong, was tied to the bleeding flesh, while the other end was fastened to the top of the pole in the middle

E   4

of the lodge. The first young man, when thus
prepared, commenced dancing around the circle
in a most frantic manner, pulling with all his
might, so as to stretch out the rope, and by his
jerking movements loosening himself by tearing
out the flesh. The young man's dance was accompanied by a chant by those who were standing around, assisted by the thumping of a hideous
drum, to keep the time. The young brave who
was undergoing this self-torture finally succeeded in tearing himself loose, and the rope
relaxed from its sudden tightness and fell back
toward the centre pole with a piece of the flesh
to which it was tied. The victim, who, up to this
point, did not move a muscle of his face, fell
down on the ground, exhausted from the pain,
which human weakness could not further conceal.
A squaw then rushed in and bore the young
brave away. He had undergone the terrible
ordeal, and amid the congratulations of the old
men, would be complimented as a warrior of
undoubted pluck and acknowledged prowess.

"Another of the young men, named Charles,
was cut in two places under the shoulder blade;
the flesh was raised with pincers, and thongs tied
around the flesh and muscles thus raised. The
thongs reached down below the knees and were
tied to buffalo skulls. With these heavy weights
dangling at the ends of the thongs, the young
man was required to dance around the circle, to

the sound of the drum and chants of the by-
standers, until the skulls became detached by
tearing out the flesh. They continued the performance until one of the skulls broke loose, but
the other remained. The mother of the young
man then rushed into the ring, leading a pony,
and tied one end of the lariat which was around
the pony's neck to the skull, which was still fastened to the young Indian. The latter then followed the pony round the ring, until nearly exhausted he fell on his face, and the skull was
thereby torn out of the flesh. The sufferer's voice
grew husky from joining in the chant; he grov-
eled on the ground in violent contortions for a
few minutes, and was then removed to the outside
of the lodge.

"A third man had the lariat of the pony hitched
to the raised muscles of his back, and was dragged
in this way several times round the ring; but the
force not being sufficient to tear loose from the
flesh, the pony was backed up, and a slack being
thus taken on the lariat, the pony was urged
swiftly forward, and the sudden jerk tore the
lariat out of the flesh."

Our informant having seen enough of these
horrid performances to satisfy his curiosity, left
with his companions, "without waiting to see the
dance through." The dance, with its bloody
orgies, lasted three whole days. This Sun Dance
is not as common as formerly, and as the Indians

settle on reservations, it is wholly done away with. The origin of the custom is uncertain.

JULESBURG.

My experience on the plains dates from September, 1867. The government ordered me to report to Fort Sedgwick, a post on the south side of the Platte River, three hundred and seventy-seven miles west of Omaha. This post lies four miles south of Julesburg, then the end of the Union Pacific Railroad. There were five thousand people there, and it was said to be the most wicked city in the world. Thieves and escaped convicts came here to gamble and lead bad lives, as they had done in Eastern cities, until driven away for fear of punishment; and often three or four would be shot down at night in drunken rows with their companions in vice and crime.

A mammoth tent was erected for a dance-house and gambling purposes. It was called "The King of the Hills," and was filled up with handsome mirrors, pianos, and furniture, and was the scene of all kinds of wickedness. It rented for six hundred dollars a day !

Here hundreds of men, engaged as freighters, teamsters, and "bull-whackers,"—as they were called, and who were in the employ of Wells, Fargo & Co. in freighting goods in large wagons to Idaho, Montana, Salt Lake, and California,— would congregate at night and gamble and ca-

rouse, spending all their three mouths' earnings,
only to go back, earn more, and spend it again in
this foolish and wicked manner.

One day I came over to the city, and while
driving from the express office, heard pistol-shots,
and soon saw the men, women, and children running in every direction. I got out of the way, fearing danger, and listened, till I had heard at least
twenty shots, and then all was stitl. I went
round to ascertain the cause, and soon found myself among a crowd of excited persons. I learned
that a bad young man had robbed a poor negro
boy of one hundred and thirty dollars he had
earned at the railroad station, and had laid it
by to go to his home in Baltimore. The fellow
denied it, and said " he'd shoot any one who
tried to arrest him." A police officer followed
him into a saloon, when the thief at once turned
and fired at the officer, wounding him in his
right elbow, so he could not reach his pistols
in his belt. But some friend handed him one,
and with it he knocked the villain down, behind
a stove. He then begged for his life, saying he
would give up the money and a thousand dollars
for his life. But it was too late. The officer shot
him in the forehead, and when I entered, he was
weltering in a pool of blood. All said, " Served
him right!" This is a law of Western life. If
two men get into a dispute, and one puts his hand
to his pocket, as if to draw a weapon, the other

E*

is sure to shoot his enemy, as the law is, *a life for a life."*

JULESBURG took its name from a small place just below Sedgwick, where a Frenchman named Jules built a ranch and raised cattle a long time before the railroad was built. Here passengers to Denver would get their meals, and the horses were changed on the stage route to Denver and to Salt Lake. Some Indians it is said killed the old man Jules, and his ranch having been taken possession of by the Indians, was shelled by cannon from Fort Sedgwick, and burned down. Mr. Greeley must remember this station, which he and Mr. Colfax and Gov. Bross, of Illinois, passed on their overland trip to California some ten years ago, and where they dined upon the universal fare,—corn-bread, coffee, and bacon.

The city of Julesburg, as it was called in 1867, was visited by a party of editors from Chicago, Cleveland, etc. They came in one of Pullman's palace cars to see the contractor of the Union Pacific Railroad lay the track, as many as four miles each day. Being anxious to write home to their papers all the wonderful things they saw and heard, they came across a strange, wild-looking man named "Sam Stanton," dressed in a buckskin suit, with a broad-brimmed hat. Sam was a returned California miner, of long experience on the plains. Him they invited to come into the beautiful car, to tell them some stories of pioneer life; and, in order to incite him, or *excite* his imagination to do so, they invited him to drink some champagne wine. As it happened, Sam had never before tasted any stimulants but common whisky, and the champagne getting into his head, made him a little tipsy.

"You want me to show you how we put out the lights in the ranches, I suppose?"

"Yes," they said; " tell us anything of Western life."

"Well, here goes," he said, and at once drew his revolver and began popping away at the beautiful globe lamps which adorned the car! Of course all the party stampeded for the door. They had had enough of Sam's stories.

It is a rule for the last one that gets into bed to put out the light; but a lazy fellow will crawl into bed and, taking aim, extinguish the light by firing off his pistol at the flame!

A "Ranch" is simply a one-story log-house, with two or three rooms, and a thatched roof of straw. Sometimes they are made of a-do-be,— a kind of dried clay-brick, such as are found in Mexico and some parts of California and Texas.

A BRAVE BOY AND SOME INDIANS.

When the railroad had been built as far as Plum Creek, two hundred and thirty miles west of Omaha, in 1866, the track-layers saw a lot of In-

dians coming toward them from over the bluffs;
and the poor Irishmen, dreading nothing so much
as the sight of a red-skin, at once took to their
heels to hide from the foe. Along with these men
were needed covered wagons, with which they
carried tools, etc., and in which at night they slept.
In one of them a boy was sitting, about twelve
or fourteen years of age. He saw nothing of the
stampede of workmen, but soon was aroused by
the yell of the Indians. He seized a Spencer
rifle lying close by him, and, putting the muzzle
through a slit of the canvas cover, took good aim
at the foremost Indian, and when within a few
yards, he shot off his rifle and felled him to the
ground. Another rode up, and met the same
fate. Several then rushed up and dragged off
the bodies of the two Indians slain, and all at
once made a quick retreat!

The Indians seeing several wagons there, supposed each one contained armed soldiers or men;
and they were quick to see that the white man's
skill was more than their bows and arrows. And
yet there was only that brave little fellow, who
saved the whole " *outfit*," and whose name ought
to be recorded as a true hero.

AN INDIAN MEAL.

Boys would be surprised to see how much an
'ndian can eat at a single meal. A " big chief"
'an eat a whole goose or turkey at one sitting.

The Indians eat right along, till they have gorged themselves and can eat no more. Perhaps it is because they seldom get what is called " a square meal," and so when plenty offers they make the most of it. One day, four chiefs of the Ar-ap-a-hoe tribe came to Fort Russell, to see about getting rations for three hundred of their tribe. They soon found their way to the commanding officer, at headquarters. He gave each one a cigar, which they puffed away at for some time. At last one of them made a motion to his mouth, signifying they were " hungry." Nearly all the tribes of wild Indians convey their ideas more by signs than by words. But the general would not take the hint. He said if he fed them once, they would come every day. A lady, however, took pity on them, and said to me, " Let us make contributions from each family, and give the poor fellows something to eat." Some brought meat, some biscuit and bread, and I made them some coffee, after inviting them to come into my yard. The children, boys and girls, assembled to see the four chiefs sitting around the table in the yard devour the food we had prepared for them.

There was no milk in the coffee, but I knew Indians were not used to it, and all things being ready, the coffee hot and the bacon smoking and smelling savory, I expected they would fall to and eat like good fellows. But I was surprised that one of them looked at the pail of coffee and gave a grunt of disapprobation. I supposed from what I had heard that an Indian would drink -coffee, swallowing the *grounds* and all. But on a close look, I discovered *about a dozen flies* were floating on top. I took a spoon and removed them, and tasting it myself, passed it round to each one in a bowl; and this time they gave another grunt,—but it was one of approbation. They ate and ate till we thought they'd split, and then asked permission to carry off in a bag what they could not stow away in their capacious stomachs!

An Indian seldom shows any signs of joy or of sorrow in any emotion whatever. But when they meet a white friend, or are surprised at anything, they exclaim, "How! how!" and shake hands all round.

An Indian trader told me at North Platte some anecdotes of their characteristics. They are all very fond of sugar, and very fond of whisky. They will often sell a buffalo robe for a bowl of sugar, and at any time would give a pony for a gallon of rye or rum.

He told me that he once saw an Indian choke a squaw to get a lump of sugar out of her mouth which he coveted ! And a storekeeper at Jules-burg (Mr. Pease) said he sold a big pup to an Indian for a robe, and the Indian seized the dog, cut his throat, and, soon as dead, threw pup into a kettle to boil up for soup !

SHALL THE INDIANS BE EXTERMINATED?

This is the cry of Western men. It is very easy to talk of " extermination." General Har- ney, an old Indian fighter, told General Sherman that a general war with the Indians would cost the government $50,000,000 a year, and stop for a long time the running of the Pacific Railroad. They fight only at an advantage,—when they out- number the whites. They fight, scatter away, and reunite again ; hide away in canons (*canyons*), gorges, and mountain fastnesses, where no soldier can find them. It would be a war of fifty years' duration.

General Sherman is reported to have said at a meeting of the Indian Peace Commissioners, at Fort Laramie, with several tribes, " Say to the head chief that President Grant loves the red men and will do all he can for them. But they must behave themselves, and if they don't, tell him *I'll kill them!*" The old chief began to mut- ter away something to himself and others.

" What does he say ?" said the general.

" Why," said the interpreter, " he says, ' *catch 'em first, then kill them !*' "

Have they never been wronged by white men ? Have you never heard of the Sand Creek massacre ?

There had been some trouble between the

Cheyennes and Arapahoes and some soldiers near Fort Lyon, in 1864, south of Denver, Colorado, where these Indians have a reservation. The origin of the trouble is uncertain. Major Anthony was sent out to fight them; but on his arrival he found them peaceable,—they had given up their prisoners and horses.

[Indians take their squaws and papooses with them when they go on hunting expeditions. The squaws prepare all the meat, dry all the game for winter food, and tan the buffalo- and deer-hides to sell. They live in tents or lodges, called "Tepees," made of tanned buffalo-skins, and usually hold about five persons, in which they cook and sleep. On the war-path, they leave their squaws and papooses in their villages. This was the case when Colonel Chivington (formerly a preacher) charged that they were hostile, as an apology for his wholesale slaughter.]

Five hundred Indians of all ages flocked, soon as attacked, to the head chief's camp,—" Black Kettle,"—and he raised the American flag, with a white truce beneath. This, you know, is respected in all civilized warfare. Then the slaughter began.

One who saw it said, " The troops (mainly volunteers) committed all manner of depredations on their victims,—scalped them, knocked out their brains. The white men used their knives, cutting squaws to pieces, clubbed little children, knocking out their brains and mutilating their

bodies in every sense of the word." Thus imi-
tating savage warfare by nominally Christian
men.

Robert Bent testified thus:

" I saw a little girl about five years of age, who
had been hid in the sand ; two soldiers discovered her, drew their pistols and shot her, and
then pulled her out of the sand by her arm," etc.

This occurred at the time government officials in Denver had sent for them,—had a " talk"
with them,—advising them to go just where they
were. Before he was killed, Black Kettle, one
of the chiefs, thus addressed the governor at
Denver :

" We have come with our eyes shut, following
Major Wynkoop's handful of men, like coming
through the fire. All we ask is, that we may
have peace with the whites. We want to hold
you by the hand. You are our father. We
have been traveling through a cloud. The sky
has been dark ever since the war began.

" These braves who are here with me, are willing to do all I say. We want to take good news
home to our people, that they may sleep in peace.

" *I have not come here with a little wolf-bark!* But
have come to talk plain with you. We must live
near the buffalo or starve. When I go home, I
will tell my people I have taken your hand, and
all of the white chiefs in Denver, and then they
will feel well, and so will all the tribes on the

F

plains, when we have eaten and drank with them."

And yet one hundred and twenty friendly Indians were all slain, and the war that followed cost $40,000,000.

A *council of Indians* was held previous to the " Chivington massacre," which stamped the character of Black Kettle, the Cheyenne chief, as noble and brave. It seems that he had purchased from an Arapahoe band two girls named Laura Roper, aged eighteen, and Belle Ewbanks, aged six years, who were captured by the Indians, after attacking Roper's ranch, on the Little Blue River, in July, 1864. Two little boys were also captured at the same time. They were carried off to the Republican River, and Black Kettle bought them for five or six ponies, to give them to their parents. Certainly a generous act. He gave them up, and met the Commissioners in council, together with several Arapahoe chiefs of small bands, all of whom were confederate together to kill the Commissioners and bring on a general war.

Black Kettle knew it, and was determined to expose the plot and break it up. But the party of white officials, with Colonel E. W. Wynkoop, were in the dark about their evil intentions. The Indians called Colonel W. " The Tall Chief that don't lie."

"BlackKettle"—Mo-ke-ta-va ta—ColonelTappan says, "was the most remarkable man of the age for magnanimity, generosity, courage, and integrity. His hospitality to destitute emigrants and travelers on the plains for years, had no limit within the utmost extent of his means; giving liberally of his stores of provisions, clothing, and horses. His fame as an orator was widely known. He was great in council, and his word was law. Hundreds of whites are indebted to him for their lives. . . . He held Colonel Chivington's men at bay for seven hours, and carried to a place of safety three hundred of his women and children,—twenty of his braves and his own wife pierced with a dozen bullets.

"Previous to the conflict, after his two brothers had been shot down and cut to pieces before his eyes (while approaching the troops to notify them of the friendly character of the Indians), he aided three white men to escape from the village, one of them a soldier. They were his guests, whom he suspected of being spies, ' but did not know it,' and they are now living to the eternal fame and honor of the chieftain. From Sand Creek he fled to the Sioux camp, where it was determined to make war upon the whites in retaliation. He protested against interfering with women and children, and insisted upon fighting the men. He was overruled. Thereupon he resigned his office as chief, and assumed the garb of a brave. He soon after made peace for his

tribe, which was faithfully kept until the burning of their village two years afterward. A war
again ensued, in which he took no part, having
promised never again to raise his hands against
the whites. He was the first to meet the Peace
Commissioners at Medicine Lodge Creek. His
many services and virtues plead like angels trum-
pet-tongued against the deep damnation of his
taking off."

Well, when the council assembled, among them
were about a dozen chiefs of Arapahoes, Cheyennes, etc.; the worst of whom was Neva,—Long-
nose,—an Arapahoe with one eye, and that a very
ugly one. He was an outlaw, commanding twenty
or thirty warriors. All were seated in a tent, and
this fellow became boisterous, and wrangled,
clamoring for a general war against all whites.
It was a most exciting time. The chiefs stripped
almost naked, and worked themselves up into a
great excitement. At last, Black Kettle rose up,
and pointing his finger at Neva, thus addressed
him :

" You, you call yourself brave ! I know what
you mean. You come here to kill these white
friends whom I have invited to come and have a
talk with us. They don't know what you mean,
but I do. You brave ! (sneeringly.) I'll tell you
what you are: your mouth is wide, so (meas-
uring a foot with his hands),—your tongue so
long (with his forefinger marking six inches on

his arm),—*and it hangs in the middle, going both ways.*
You're a coward, and dare not fight me." Here
all the Indians gave a grunt of approbation.
"Now, go," said he, "and begone! This council is broken up; I have said it; you hear my
words; begone!" And they slunk off, completely
cowed down.

Dog-soldiers were with them, well equipped
for a big fight, and these white men beguiled,
would all have been slain only for Mo-ke-ta-va-ta.
A " dog-soldier" is a youth who has won, gradu-
ally, by successful use of the bow and arrow, a
position to use the gun, and stand to the warriors
just as our police force do to us, in guarding
property, etc. These boys have a stick, called a
" coo," on which they make a notch for everything they kill,—a kind of tally,—and when the
coo is of a certain length, they are promoted to
the rank of a " dog-soldier."

INDIANS DON'T BELIEVE HALF THEY HEAR.

When several chiefs are allowed to visit Washington on errands for their tribes, to get more
given them, they tell their people how numerous
are the children of their Great Father they have
met on their way, and what big guns they saw,
etc. But those at home believe it is a lie, gotten
up by the " white man's medicine," as they call
it. All have heard of a young chief whose

F*   5

father gave a stick, on which he should cut a notch for every white man he met. But it soon got full, and he threw it away.

The most amusing experience is told of a lot of Indians having been induced to go into a photographer's and have their likenesses taken. The operator asked a chief to look at his squaw (sitting for her phiz) through the camera. It looks as though one was sitting, or rather standing on his head,—reversing one's position. The chief was very angry at seeing his squaw in such an uncomely attitude, and he walked over and beat her. She denied it, but he saw it. He looked again, and again she was turned upside down. He said it was the white man's medicine, and would have nothing to do with it!

An Indian boy was asked some questions by one of the Peace Commissioners about some trouble, and he said to a chief, "Does the boy tell the truth?"

"Yes," replied the chief, "you may believe what he says; he never saw a white man before!"

ARMY OFFICERS.

The army officers are generally friends of the Indians. They are certainly, as a rule, just to the well-behaved Indians, and ready to sacrifice their lives in punishing bad ones.

General W. S. Harney, a retired army officer,

is among the most noted. His life will be a most interesting one, full of adventure with the red men. General Harney graduated at West Point when nineteen years old, was sent out to the frontier, where he has lived fifty years. Grown gray in their companionship, and cradled in experience with the Indian tribes, says "I never knew an Indian chief to break his word!"

Major-General George H. Thomas, who commanded at Camp Cooper, Texas, some ten years ago, made a forced march of a hundred miles, with one hundred and twenty cavalry, to protect a village of Comanches from Baylor and three thousand rangers that were marching to destroy them. General Thomas was successful. He then marched in rear of the Indians hundreds of miles to shield them from the Texans. This gallant and chivalric officer died with a reputation dear to our country.

Major-General John Sedgwick, who fell during the war of the rebellion, rendered similar services on the plains, in defense of the Arapahoes, at about the same time; and Colonel Edward W. Wynkoop, five years later, in behalf of the Cheyennes.

Other officers might be mentioned for similar services, among them Generals Z. Taylor, W. S. Harney, and Alfred H. Terry. The last mentioned, two years ago, with a strong head, heart, and hand, squelched a conspiracy in Montana to exterminate the Crow Indians. Again, the next summer, flying across the plains, and up the Missouri River as fast as steam could carry him, to rescue a Sioux village from the border settlers. This splendid officer was removed from the command of the Department of Dakota, to make room for Hancock.

Captain Silas S. Soule, in Colorado, a few years ago, and Lieutenant Philip Sheridan, in Oregon, ten years since, might also be referred to in this connection, as drawing their swords in defense of the Indians and the right.

WHAT SHALL BE DONE?

The question is, How can the problem be solved, so as to best protect and secure the rights of the Indians, and at the same time promote the welfare of both races?

Within the memory of the writer, the tomahawk once reflected the light of burning cabins along the Tennessee, Ohio, Illinois, and Missouri Rivers, and the scalping-knives dripped with the blood of our border settlers, as we have driven the Indians back, back, to the setting sun !

But behold the change to-day, where the church has missions, and the red men are treated like immortal beings, with souls to be saved.

Mr. Wm. Welsh says of what he saw in Nebraska: "The blanket and bow discarded; the spear is broken, and the hatchet and war-club lie buried. The skin-lodge (tepee) has given place to the cottage and the mansion. Among the Santee Sioux, on Niobrara River, in Nebraska, the Episcopal Church has a mission, where one can see the murderous weapons and the conjuror's charms, by aid of which the medicine-man wrought his fiendish arts.

" That is the *pipe-stem*,—never smoked except on the war-path,—always blackened, being associated with deeds of darkness.

" These," he says, " are laid at the feet of our Christian missionaries, such as Bishops Whipple and Clarkson, and Rev. Mr. Hinman ; where school-houses abound, and the feet of many thousand little children, thirsting after knowledge, are seen entering those vestibules of science ; while churches, consecrated to the Christian's God, reflect for miles the sun's rays, tokens of a brighter light to their darkened heathen souls !

"Dear children, thanks to our holy religion, a few faithful men, taking their lives in their hands, have gone forth at the church's call,—bearing precious seed,—struggled and toiled, endured severe privations, afflictions, and trials, and saved in tears the germs of light, truth, and hope, which to-day have ripened into a glorious harvest of intelligence and Christian civilization ! Christ said, ' It must needs be that offenses come, but woe unto that man by whom the offense cometh.' "

Now, if the wrongs accumulated, done to the poor, ignorant pagan Indians for years and years since the Mayflower landed her pilgrims on these shores, are to be redressed in this world (for there is no repentance for nations after), and if a God of justice so require that we atone to them, or suffer greater torments from their children, who shall say it is not a righteous retribution?

If we find them fierce, hostile, and revengeful, if they are cruel, and sometimes perpetrate atrocities that sicken the soul, and almost paralyze us with horror,—burning and pillaging,—let us remember that two hundred and fifty years of injustice, oppression, and wrong, heaped upon them by *our* race, with cold, calculating, and relentless perseverance, have filled them with the passion of revenge and made them desperate. If you and I, boys, were Indians, we would do just as Indians do. *Their tender mercies are cruel, but there is a reason why it is so.*

The former Indian agents, on a salary of eighteen hundred dollars a year, got very rich in a short time. How could they do so but by swindling the poor Indians, who have no idea of the relative value of money, or the cost of goods?

Not long since a tribe just above us was paid off their annuities in shoddy blankets; they were bought back again with whisky, and another tribe was paid with the same blankets; and one agent took out several thousand " elastics" (girls know what I mean) to pay the Indians (among other things), and yet no wild Indian ever wore a stocking!

Again, as the Indian is crowded back beyond the tide of emigration, and hanging like the froth of the billows upon the very edge is generally a host of law-defying whites, who introduce among the Indians every form of demoralization and disease with which depraved humanity in its most degraded form is afflicted. These the Indian see more of than anybody else (except the military, whom they look upon mostly as protectors), as good people come along, the Indian must *push on*, still farther toward the setting sun!

A GOOD JOKE BY LITTLE RAVEN.

Little Raven, an Arapahoe chief, laughed heartily when we told him something about heaven and hell; remarking, "All good men—white and red men—would go to heaven; all bad men, white or red, would go to hell." Inquiring the cause of his merriment when he had recovered his breath, he said, "I was much pleased with what you say of those two places, and the kind of people that will go to each when they come to die. It is a good notion,—heap good,—for if all the whites are like the ones I know, when Indian gets to heaven but few whites will trouble him there; pretty much all go to t'other place !"

HOW THE INDIAN IS CHEATED.

It is true, as General Harney remarked, "Better to board and lodge them at the Fifth Avenue Hotel than to fight them, as a matter of economy." Besides depleting the Indian appropriation fund, voted annually by Congress, of millions of dollars, but which was used to carry on elections, and the Indian got what was left; which may be compared to cheese-parings and cheese, or skim-milk and cream. The Indian gets the parings and the skim-milk !

The Quaker agents, as they are called, are doing a good work, because they see that honest dealings are had with the annuities paid them. If the President had done little else, this feature of reform will redound to his credit forever.

BURIAL OF A CHIEF'S DAUGHTER.

Spotted Tail, the head chief of the Brule Sioux, sent a request to the commanding officer at Fort Laramie, saying "his daughter had died in Powder River country (fifteen days' journey), and had begged her father to have her grave made among the whites." Consent was given, she having been known to the officers for several years, and her death was brought on by exposure to the hardships of wild Indian life, and also from grief, that her tribe would go to war.

He was met outside the " Post" by the officers, with the honors due his station. The officer in command spoke in words of comfort, saying, " he sympathized with him, and was pleased at this mark of confidence in committing to his care the remains of his loved child. The Great Spirit had taken her, and he never did anything except for some good purpose. Everything should be prepared for the funeral at sunset, and as the sun went down, it might remind him of the darkness left in his lodge when his daughter was taken away; but as the sun would surely rise again, so she would rise, and some day we would all meet in the land of the Great Spirit."

The chief exhibited great emotion at these words, and shed tears; a thing quite unusual in an Indian. He took the hand of the officer and said, " This must be a dream for me to be in such a fine room, and surrounded by such as you. ,Have I been asleep during the last four years of hardship and trial, dreaming that all is to be well again ? or is this real ? Yes, I see that it is,—the beautiful day, the sky blue, without a cloud ; the wind calm and still, to suit the errand I came on, and remind me that you offer me peace ! We think we have been much wronged, and entitled to compensation for dam-

G

age done and distress caused by making so many
roads through our country, driving and destroying the buffalo and game. My heart is very sad,
and I cannot talk on business. I will wait and
see the counselors the Great Father will send."

The scene, it is added, was the most impress-
ive I ever saw, and all the Indians were awed
into silence. A scaffold was erected (see print)
at the cemetery, and a coffin was made. Just
before sunset, the body was carried, followed by
the father and other relatives, with chaplain,*
officers, soldiers, and Indians. The chaplain read
the beautiful burial-service, interpreted by another
to them.

One said, "I can hardly describe my feelings
at witnessing here this first Christian burial of an
Indian, and one of such consideration among her
tribe. The hour, the place, the solemnity, even
the restrained weeping of the mother and other
relatives, all combined to affect me deeply."

It is added: the officers, to gratify Monica's
father, each placed an offering in her coffin.
Colonel Maynadier, a pair of gauntlets, to keep
her hands warm (it was winter), Mr. Bullock gave
a handsome piece of red cassimere to cover the
coffin. To complete the Indian ceremony, her
two milk-white ponies were killed and their
heads and tails nailed on the coffin. These ponies

---

* Rev. A. Wright, post-chaplain, U. S. A.

the Indians supposed she would ride again in the hunting-grounds whither she had gone.

AN INDIAN RAID ON SIDNEY STATION, UNION PACIFIC RAILROAD.

In the month of April, 1868, while returning from the East, we took dinner at Sidney Station, on the railroad, four hundred and fourteen miles west of Omaha, at noon. While we were there, two freight conductors brought in their trains and dined at the same time we did, and when we started they were on the platform and said good-by to us. They concluded to go out a fishing, a mile or two from the settlement, behind one of the bluffs. We had not left on our way to Cheyenne more than about an hour, when we learned by telegraph at "Antelope Station" (thirty-seven miles), that a band of twenty or thirty Sioux Indians had come suddenly upon the two conductors, named Cahoone and Kinney, and, after a severe conflict, had shot both through with arrows, and scalped one of them (Cahoone), besides killing some of the railroad hands at work repairing the road near by the scene of conflict. Presently we met a special train, consisting of engine and caboose-car, coming with tremendous speed,—one mile a minute,—containing Dr. Latham, surgeon of the railroad from Cheyenne. It seems that the soldiers—a small company—were completely surprised, and not being mounted, could only protect the station, but could not follow up the Indians to punish them for their audacity.

There were nearly two hundred and fifty people, including one hundred infantry soldiers, at the station; and the alarm of " Indians" being given, the whole population turned out with such arms as they could lay hold of. The sight of so many persons disconcerted the Indians, and they checked their horses within a respectable distance of the station. About two hundred shots were fired,—many of them in the wildest manner, and mostly hurting nobody.

The Indians rode round the upper side of Sidney—*i.e.* west—after the affray with the conductors, and attacked the section-men, circling round and round (as usual in their mode of Indian warfare, to draw out the fire of their enemies, till they exhaust their ammunition), till they had killed several of the poor Irishmen at work. These men had with them a hand-car, and the boss had a rifle with him, and only one charge or cartridge in his gun. He did the best he could, however, by jumping on the car and taking aim at his enemies, and keeping the gun pointed towards them, while the men worked the hand-car safe into Sidney Station. He escaped with his life, and several of his comrades.

These two conductors had about seven arrows

shot into each of them, several going right through their bodies, and which had to be broken off to draw them out. One—Thomas Cahoone—was scalped twice, on the top and back of his head. The other—William Kinney— kept his captor at bay by a pistol he had, and thus aiming at the Indian, saved his hair. Both were brought up carefully in the caboose-car to Cheyenne, and next day I saw them under Dr. Latham's treatment. All thought that both would surely die, but both got well; and the one who was scalped is now living at a station on the Union Pacific Railroad. It is a terrible opera-tion to be scalped, and few survive it. But, thanks to the surgeon's skill, these men are living, and feel very much like taking vengeance on their tormentors,—*if they ever catch them!*

WHY DO INDIANS SCALP THEIR ENEMIES?

I have been a good deal puzzled to know the origin of this custom, of always scalping a foe in battle, both among themselves and in fighting white people. A negro is never scalped by the Indians. In conversing with Major A. S. Burt, of 9th United States Infantry, at our post, who has had much experience among the Indians on the plains, I learn some things which give a clue to the matter, which agree with all I can hear. He says that each Indian wears a " scalp-lock"

G*

(see engraving), which is a long tuft of hair, into which the Indian inserts his medicine, which consists generally of a few quills of eagle's feathers. This "*medicine*" is simply a "*charm*," as we call it, gotten by purchase of the medicine-man of the tribe. The medicine-man is the most influential man in each tribe. He professes to be able to conjure, by his arts and influence with the Great Spirit, certain articles, which he sells to the Indians of his tribe. This "medicine" the superstitious believe will cure diseases, and help him against his enemy in battle. Hence, in scalping a fallen foe, the victor deprives him of his charm, and shows it in triumph, as a token of his skill in battle. If you visit an Indian in his tent, and ask him to show you his "medicine," he will do so, if you pay him in such things as he needs to make therewith a feast, both for himself and an offering to his medicine idol; but as the idol can't eat, it goes of course into the stomach of the live Indian !*

Another idea: the Indian believes that the spirit of the enemy he slays enters into himself, and he is thereby made the stronger; hence *he slays all that he can.* I have seen young warriors

---

* The Indian keeps his " medicine" hung up in his tent, and prays to it,—dreams about it,—and if his dream is of good luck, he acts accordingly. This applies to hunting, going on war expeditions, etc.; in short, it is his sort of saint, to which he pays idolatrous worship.

in the streets of Cheyenne, with their hair reaching down almost to their heels; and all along it
you'd see strung round pieces of silver, from
the size of a silver dollar to a tea-saucer; each
one of which was a tell-tale of the number of
the scalps the young fellow had taken. It was
what the ladies would call a " waterfall !"

Speaking of this, as revealing the pride of
Indians in showing their prowess, I learned of
a *young buck*, coming into a post and walking
round, dressed in the top of Indian fashion,—*i.e.*
with paint on his face, feathers in his hair, and
brass ornaments on his leggins. These young
fellows put on all the gewgaws they can to make
a show of importance. Well, he finally walked
into the post-trader's store, and asked Mr. Bullock if he didn't think it made the officers *faint*
when they saw him ? " Yes," said he, " I think
you'd better take off some of your things (pointing to his trappings), they will scare somebody."

INDIAN BOY'S EDUCATION.

When an Indian gets to be eighteen years old,
it is expected that he will strike out for himself,
and do some act to show his bravery; and that
begins in striking somebody to kill them (a white
or Indian of a hostile tribe), and to steal stock, a
horse, or mule, or cattle.

No young warrior can get a wife till he has

taken the scalp of a white man or Indian, and have stolen a horse or pony. This being a law of the Sioux, so in proportion as he scalps and steals horses so does his number of wives increase, and the greater a warrior does he become. In short, he becomes " a big heap chief." What to us becomes a murder or a theft,—the very first act of a young Indian,—in his own tribe is a great and praiseworthy deed. So you see what blood has been shed, and other acts of cruelty caused by Spotted Tail, Red Cloud, and others, who have imbrued their hands in the blood of innocent victims with a fiendish delight that savages only know and take pleasure in.

As the arrows tell of the tribe to which they belong,—colored near the end,—green for the Sioux, blue, Cheyenne, red or brown, Arrapahoes, black feathers, Crow,—so the tribe to which an Indian murderer belongs is known by the method (usually) by which the victim is scalped. The Cheyennes remove a piece not larger than a silver dollar from immediately over the left ear; the Arrapahoes take the same from over the right ear. Others take from the crown, forehead, or nape of the neck. The Utes take the entire scalp from ear to ear, and from forehead to nape of neck.

MAKING PRESENTS.

A grocer in Julesburg had married a squaw; after awhile she left him and joined her tribe. Coming that way again, she came and looked in upon her former husband at the back-door, while all her relations stood staring around to see if she would be welcomed back again. But he took no notice of her. One of his friends said to him, "Joe, why don't you go and call her in, you know you are glad to see her back again; you certainly want her?"

"No, no," said he, "I ain't going to make any fuss over her at all. If I do, the whole crowd of her relations, uncles, aunts, and cousins, will come in to shake hands, and congratulate me with 'How, how,' expecting each one to have a pound of sugar. No, no, you don't catch me."

INDIANS MAKING SIGNALS.

The Indians can make signals to the distance of eight or ten miles to their confederates. This is done in two ways: first, by lighting one or more fires; secondly, by flashing the sunlight by small mirrors from one bluff to another. Thus, by day or by night, they can communicate at great distances. They have "field-glasses" also. If an Indian is benighted on the plains, he can

6

make himself quite comfortable, where a white man would perish in the winter with cold. He will gather some buffalo chips, and strike a fire with a flint, sitting close to it, and throwing his blanket around him in shape of a tent, and let the smoke go out of a hole at the top. He thus looks at night like a stump on fire.

MERCIFUL INDIANS.

A poor old German was traveling in Colorado with his wagon, when he was set upon by a lot of Indians. They drew their bows to shoot him, when he dropped upon his knees and began to pray vehemently. " Oh," said he, " mine goot friends, please don't shoot me! I'm joost the best friends what you have got. I never killed not nobody, and please don't shoot a poor fellow like me." The Indians did not understand a word he said, but he acted in such a ludicrous manner, they thought he was crazy, and so they let him pass unharmed. They seemed to have a sense of the ludicrous, as they went off laughing at the poor Dutchman quite heartily.

A SCENE AT NORTH PLATTE.

After the treaty with the Indians at Fort Laramie, in 1868, the Peace Commission adjourned, part to go with General Sherman to

New Mexico, a part to meet at Fort Rice, Dakota, with General Terry, part to go up to Fort
Bridger, in Wyoming, with General Augur, and
another with Commissioner Taylor at North
Platte, Nebraska, to meet different tribes not
present at Laramie. There I went to see Spotted
Tail's band, and learn all I could of Indian
life. Spotted Tail was off on the Republican
River, in Kansas, hunting buffalo with White
Bear and Man-who-owns-his-Horses, nephew
of Spotted Tail. Mr. Goodell, of Chicago, was
there, to see if he could not induce the Indians
to undertake the weaving of blankets and shawls,
etc. by hand-looms, such as are in use in the Ohio
Penitentiary. I went with him to hear what they
would say. Rolled up in a blanket were speci-
mens of woolen yarn of bright colors, and a piece
of cloth partly woven, and he had a picture of a
girl sitting at the loom in the act of weaving.
Around us gathered all the young squaws, who
expressed great delight at the whole thing and
seemed to comprehend it; while young Indian
lads stood at a distance and only gave a grunt of
qualified satisfaction, or reservation. I should
think there would be no difficulty in introducing
such work, as the squaws will readily labor on
anything that promises to add to their comfort
or adornment of their persons.

Then quite an amusing incident occurred,
which I must relate, though the joke was upon

myself, or my friend, Mr. G——. Seeing a tall young squaw standing in front of her tent, I said, "Let us go and see what she is doing." She had made her morning toilet, and was very prettily dressed in gay colors, with a long red shawl on, coming down to her feet. I should say the entrance to the tepees or tents is through a hole hidden by a round hoop, covered with deer-skin, hanging by a string only, so as to be thrust aside easily when one wants to enter.

I said to her, " Me wa-se-na-cha-wa-kon!" That is to say, I am a medicine-man, or minister of the Great Spirit. " Wa-kon" means Great Spirit. Looking first at me, then at Mr. G——, she raised her finger and said, " Me no want." Then she turned and rushed into her tent,—shot in like a prairie-dog into his hole,—leaving us to feel rather silly by being so suddenly " cut" by a young beauty on the plains. I said, " Mr. G——, she evidently don't like your good looks or mine," and we walked off quite mortified. The interpreter explained her conduct, saying she was not " sick," and therefore did not want any " charm" to make her well.

Here I saw an Indian child, five years old, dressed in a most elegant suit of buckskin, embroidered with beads and horse-hair of various colors. The frock came below the knees, with a handsome fringe at the bottom, and underneath the little fellow wore leggins and moccasins. I

never saw any child dressed so beautiful or looking like a little prince, as he was, of the tribe. I
would have given fifty dollars for the " outfit," if
I had a child to wear it. How is it that these rude
children of nature can do such beautiful bead-
work,—all of the figures as regular as if laid out
by geometrical rule,—or as perfect as any lady
could make the figures of an afghan ?

This station of the Union Pacific Railroad is
just beyond the crossing of the Platte River, of
half a mile in width.

It is an important little place of a few hundred
people, on account of the machine-shops and
round-house for locomotives, and as one of the
main points where Indians cross from Dakota to
the Republican River when on hunting expeditions. Hence a company of soldiers are stationed
here to protect the railroad and the long bridge
just east of the town. All along the road, at
each station, are troops also for protection, who
usually " turn out," range in file, and " present
arms" as the train approaches.

Here we met a white man named Pratt,—that
is to say, if he were washed in the river he would
look white,—who said that he had lived with the
tribe for sixteen years, and had nine (half-breed)
children, and they were more filthy and squalid
than those of any other lodge.

A squaw had died here, and was buried as
usual, by elevating the body upon upright poles.

H

A stock of food was left with her at night, to eat on the way to the other country. But lo! in the morning she came down and ate it all up, saying to her friends, "She wanted to see her aunt before departing." She lived a week longer, and died, as it was supposed, again. It is said that her friends got tired of such fooling, and being determined to end the matter, adopted the white man's mode of covering her up in the ground! Again she rose up and preferred some new request; but thinking the old enchantress had stayed long enough this side the hunting-grounds, they forced her down and laid sufficient turf upon her to keep her quiet for a long last sleep.

Among the Pawnees at Columbus, on the reservation near the railroad, an Indian trader makes a good thing out of the poor fellows in this way:

For instance, the Indian Bureau pays off the tribe twice a year. In the spring, blankets, etc.; these are worth at least three dollars each. The Indians sell these blankets for a double handful of coffee and sugar. Then they buy them back in the fall with money and buffalo meat, which they sell to the trader at six cents the pound. He then cures the meat and sells it back to them for twenty-five cents the pound; thus making nine per cent. on it. Some one, it is said, complained to the government about it, and they sent a new agent to them; but the Pawnees had confidence in the old agent or trader named Platt, and they stoutly refused to trade with the new man!

ACROSS THE PLAINS.

When Vice-President Colfax and Horace Greeley, and Governor Bross of Illinois, made the journey overland to California, about twelve years since, they went all the way by stage from the Missouri River to Denver, Colorado, to Salt Lake, etc., through the mountains of the Sierra Nevada. It took them about thirty days to go. Mr. Greeley said he " could think of these plains (called in your maps the 'Great American Desert') as fit for nothing but to fill up between commercial cities!" But he was partly mistaken, as his friends are now planting a colony (named Greeley) of intelligent settlers on the Cach-le-pow-dre Creek, south of Cheyenne, fifty-five miles toward Denver, where ninety thousand acres of land have been secured for tillage, and where saw-mills and stores and dwellings are to be erected. The success of this enterprise has led to another one. The railroad *has projected civilization one hundred years ahead*, opening up a highway for commerce from New York to the " Golden Gate," to Asia, Africa, and China, which will astonish the world and divert the course of trade to the Pacific coast.

But you are interested mainly, I see, in reading

about the incidents which attended the opening up of this great national highway.

The dangers attending the building of the road were sometimes very great, as the Indians saw very plainly that it was the white man's encroachment on his hunting-grounds. And when even the telegraph-poles were being put up, long before, the Indians imagined that the government was thus putting them up to fence off their hunting-grounds, so they could not get any more buffalo! And once, after I came to Fort Sedgwick, the wires were said to be " down," and no communication could be had with other posts in the upper country. It was feared that the Indians had been tampering with the wires, and torn them down. But the operators went out under an escort of soldiers to see what the difficulty was. They came back again in a couple of days, and reported that the Indians had not meddled with the wires at all. But it seemed that some buffaloes in a large drove had taken the privilege of scratching their rumps against the poles, and thus tore them down ; and getting their horns entangled in the wires, the wild creatures had carried off about four miles of telegraph-wire !

WHY DOES NOT THE INDIAN MEDDLE WITH THE
TELEGRAPH ?

It is said that the pioneer company over the
plains got together several chiefs and explained
as well as they could the *modus operandi* of ob-
taining electricity from the clouds, and making
it useful in conveying intelligence to great distances. This was hard for them to believe, because they are superstitious, and attribute all
phenomena they do not fully understand to *con-
juration* or *charms*, such as their medicine-man
practices. However, they concluded to put the
matter to a test.

So it was that two principal Indians, about
one hundred miles apart, agreed to send a message over the lines on a given day, and then they
would travel toward each other as fast as they
could to see if the message (known only to themselves and the operator) should be correct. Of
course it proved as we would expect, and they
were satisfied. This intelligence has spread from
one tribe to another, and they, believing that it is
somehow (as it is in truth) connected with the
Great Spirit who controls the winds and the
storms; hence they do not meddle with it.

H*

PLUM CREEK MASSACRE.

But it is not to be supposed that the Indians quietly submitted to the building of the railroad through their country.

The most formidable obstacle which was met with in building the road occurred in 1866, by the throwing off the track a train of cars at Plum Creek, near the Platte River, two hundred and thirty miles west of Omaha.

The Indians were led on by a half-breed, and probably one or more scalawag whites were en-gaged in this diabolical act, as one was found among the killed with his face painted black and wearing Indian clothing. Some one having a fertile imagination made a picture of this scene, and I saw it copied in Philadelphia for some wall-paper to ornament hotel dining-rooms. Speak-ing to some ladies there about the delightful trip to California over the Pacific Railroad, one ex-claimed, " I would like to visit California, but oh, my! I never could venture on the danger. Just look at the picture in the window, corner Chestnut Street and Broad. The horrid Indians have thrown the cars off the track, and killing all the passengers !" I explained to her that it was a fancy sketch entirely, gotten up for a bar-room wall-paper, and that it was ridiculous and false ; for the picture was made to show the loco-motive off the rail, and the Indians riding round the cars in white shirt sleeves and bright-red, flaring neckties, like gay cavaliers or brigands !

PAWNEE INDIANS—YELLOW SUN AND BLUE HAWK.

Both these Indians declare themselves innocent of the crime of murder. I visited Omaha in the fall of 1869, where they were lodged in jail awaiting their trial. Just before I came one of them had escaped, and gone back to the Pawnee reservation, near Columbus. Here the sheriff an'd soldiers found him with his squaw, decked out in all their style of paint and ornament, ready for the sacrifice. He was ready and willing to be slain *among* his own people, but to go back and suffer the ignominy of being hung up by the neck till dead was more than he could bear. If the Indian dies in this way, all believe they cannot enter into the happy hunting-grounds.

They were supposed to have murdered Edward McMurty, near Grand Island, Nebraska, in June, 1868.

After being shut up in a filthy jail about two years, they were acquitted. This was a sample of the way we dispense justice in our courts of law.

This post was established a great many years
since by the American Fur Company, to trade
with the Indians, buying furs and peltries of them
in return for various articles of merchandise, such
as tobacco, sugar, coffee, blankets, calico, beads,
etc. Mr. John Jacob Astor, the millionaire of
New York, made his great wealth by dealing in
furs with the Indians.

It is related of an agent of the company that
while weighing the furs, he would place his foot
on the scales and call it a pound! Of course he
could keep it on as long as he chose, and the
Indians would be none the wiser. It is a good
story, but in nowise related to Mr. Astor, who was
reputed to be honest, and at one time very poor.

It was full of curiosity that I started from Fort
Russell with the paymaster, Major Burbank, In-
spector-General Sweitzer, Medical Director J.
B. Brown, and others, on the last of May, 1870,
with an escort of a dozen cavalry, to pay a few
days' visit to Laramie, ninety-five miles northeast of our post. Leaving at noon in procession,
with three ambulances and as many army wagons,
scaling the bluffs, bare of everything like trees
or shrubs, and only covered with grass and wild
flowers, and now and then sage-bush and prickly-
pear cactus, which are very troublesome to the
horses' feet. The roads were, as usual, very hard

and fine, so that up hill and down dale we made
six miles to the hour all the way. Our first
station was Horse Creek, twenty-five miles,
where we camped on a fine stream of water for
the night. When a party thus camps out, the
wagons are corraled, as it is called,—*i.e.* a circle
is made of them and the horses are tethered inside
or *lariated* with a rope long enough to let them
feed, and this is held by an iron stake or pin
driven into the ground. Then the tents are put
up in a line, and at once begins the work of
gathering brush and sticks (or buffalo-chips),
with which to cook a savory supper of bacon,
potatoes, and hot coffee. This is the time for
cracking jokes, telling stories of pioneer life,—
and the colored boys are full of fun. We had
one from the South named Tom Williams, belonging to Colonel Mason, of the 5th Cavalry.
After enjoying our evening meal and getting
ready to lie down in our tents, spread on the
grass, as the evening approached, the sun was
sinking behind Laramie Peak,—a mountain far
away in the Black Hills, towering up eight thousand feet,—and all nature was hushed into repose,
and each one with his lungs full of the light air,
and his body weary with a long ride, just drop-
ping off to sleep,—all at once there was a yell
and halloo outside, which caused me to jump up
and look out to see if any red-skins had broke
through the guard and invaded our peaceful

circle. Instead of scalping Sioux, there was nothing the matter but the return of a drove of large beef-cattle we had passed grazing on the Chugwater, and which sought our camping-ground on account of a bare place where they could lie down and be warm for the night. Our Tom was racing up and down among them, yelling "Hi, hi!" and shaking his blanket in all directions to stampede the poor cattle, who had as good a right as we to the soil.

Pickets were stationed all around us, and, save the snoring of some tired sleeper and the occasional braying of a mule or two, we slept soundly, with no fear of Indians. Here we met a white man and his wife, a squaw, and several others, who were waiting for Red Cloud and his chiefs, who were on their way to Washington from Fort Fetterman. They were related to John Reichaud, a half-breed belonging to Red Cloud's party. This Reichaud had lived about Laramie and Fetterman for many years, and, by raising stock and trading, had accumulated, it is said, about two hundred thousand dollars. During last winter, while drunk, he quarreled with a soldier, and a little while after, in passing some barracks at Fetterman, he aimed his revolver at a soldier, who was sitting in front of his quarters, named Kernan, and killed him, supposing it was the same soldier he had just before been quarreling with. Finding out his mistake, he fled away up to Red

Cloud's camp, and while there incited the Indians
to make war upon the whites. At the time we
were going up, General John E. Smith was
journeying towards us with Red Cloud and his
band of warriors, and having Reichaud as the
chief's prisoner. It was said he expected to get
the President to pardon him and allow him to
establish a trading-post for the Ogallallas. The
feeling against this outlaw was such as to make
General Smith fear that some one at Cheyenne
would shoot him, and so the party turned off to
Pine Bluff Station, about forty-three miles east
of that town. We thus missed seeing them. But
there were other objects of interest in our journey, and we went on to the mail station, called
the Chug, a place not of much note,—for beside
a company of cavalry, there were not a dozen
ranches there on the beautiful stream, along
whose banks were growing willow-trees, and the
cottonwood also. Besides, there were half a
dozen tepees filled with half-breeds, who are
herders and wood-choppers in the mountains.

While the paymaster was dispensing the green-
backs to Uncle Sam's boys, the doctor and I sal-
lied out with a guide in search of those much
admired

MOSS AGATES,

which are here found in great abundance, even
quarried out of a bluff and carried off by the
wagon-load. The guide had been there but once,

and somehow or other he could not locate it exactly, and we had a ride out of six miles and back without finding the spot. Still, we picked up a few on the way. As these are now so much the fashion for jewelry, I will describe them. First, I should say that most suppose they contain real moss, or fern-leaves, so distinct are they seen in a clear agate to resemble them. Thus you see imitations of pine-trees, vines, a deer's head, and sprigs of various kinds; but it is through iron solutions penetrating them when in a soluble state. If you take a pen and drop some ink into a tumbler of water, it will scatter and form for the moment an appearance like a moss agate. These agates, when found on bluffs or dry places, are coated over with a white covering of lime or alkali. Those in the beds of rivers found along the line of the Pacific Railroad, are smooth and transparent. They are called the " Cheyenne brown agate," " Granger water agate," " Church Buttes light-blue agate," and the " Sweet-water agate."

There are great quantities of them near Church Butte and Granger stations, nearly nine hundred miles west of Missouri River. You have to poke among cobble-stones, etc. to find them, and when a person comes upon a handsome specimen, he will shout, as did a minister from Chicago, one day, with me, when he picked up a nice one as large as an egg,—" Glory hallelujah !"

It is like searching for gold and silver,—very exciting, and far more pleasurable than fishing or hunting. A friend here has about sixty pounds of agates, for which he was offered by a lapidary in New York five dollars a pound. A handsome stone for a ring or pin is worth, when cut into shape, from three to five dollars. The lapidary cuts them with a steel wheel, about eight inches in diameter, using oil and diamond-dust in cutting and polishing.

A YOUNG BRAVE.

At Chug Station I met a frontiersman named Phillips, of long experience, who told me in his new adobe house of an old chief who had lost five sons, and when the first was slain he cut off a piece of his thumb, next of his forefinger, and so on, till five told of his boys killed. The last was a brave, and supposed no ball could hit him, wearing, he supposed, "a charmed life." He came to the " Chug" and dared them to shoot. As he and three or four more had killed a white man and wounded others, the people all turned out, and Phillips shot the bold young fellow, and wounded the rest of the party so that they died. The body of the young Indian lay by the road-side for several weeks, till the wolves and ravens had picked his bones, and I picked up his skull, pierced through with several balls, to bring back and present to the post-surgeon.

This grinning skull was lying on the grass which covered the roadside, and almost beneath towering monuments or bluffs of sandstone, which jut out at several points on the road, running along for great distances, and towering up several hundred feet high. We passed soon after several of these projections, which look like fortifications and baronial castles of some knights of the olden time. "Chimney Rock" is well known to travelers as a series of fluted columns, and standing solitary, as sentinels in the desert, they look solemn, lonely, and sublime. Old George, the stage-driver, has passed them twice a week for many years, and the wonder is he has not lost his scalp.

Sometimes the chiefs and old Indians will cut slits in their cheeks and rub ashes in them, sitting over the fire and bemoaning the loss of their dead children. They present a horrid appearance to one who looks at their pagan mode of bewailing the departed.

Arrived at Fort Laramie on the third day, we were courteously welcomed by Colonel F. F. Flint, of the 4th Infantry, commandant of the post. Delicacy dictates that we forbear to speak of the charming family which surrounds him; but the rarity of Christian households in the army made our visit there like to an oasis in the desert.

To visit the Indian graves surrounding the

post was a prominent object before us in going.
Lieutenant Theodore F. True, with an orderly,
two mules, and a horse saddled, found us fording
the Laramie River to inspect the grave,—if such
it can be called, as shown in the picture on this
page,—where the body was dried up like a
mummy, and nothing else but fragments of a
buffalo-robe dangling in the wind was to be seen.
Relic hunters had carried away everything in the
shape of bow and arrow, wampum, etc.

We moralized over this beautiful feature of
Indian superstition, wherein they are certainly
free from the horrid thought that any one is ever
buried alive !

Next we sought the place where the remains
of Mon-i-ca, daughter of Zin-ta-gah-lat-skah, was
placed, by her request, in the white man's cemetery, and alongside of the body of her uncle
Sho-ta,—" Old Smoke,"—an old warrior. The
coffin was made at the post, and elevated on posts
about ten feet high. They cover these coffins
with handsome red broadcloth, and deposit in
each all the trinkets and valuables belonging to
the departed. One other grave there the Indians
visit annually, and mourn over with their lamen-
tations,—that of a Frenchman named Sublette,
who brought them down and directed them how
to vanquish their enemies, the Pawnees, in a
great battle.

THE HEAD CHIEF—RED CLOUD.

Red Cloud is regarded as the head chief of the Sioux nation, and for over twenty years has been thus venerated. He is fifty-three years old, and claims to have fought in eighty-seven battles, often wounded, but never badly hurt. Red Cloud is about six feet six inches in his stock-ings (I mean moccasins), large features, high cheek bones, and a big mouth, and walks knock-kneed, as others do. His face is painted, and his ears pierced for gaudy rings, which men and women have an equal pride for. His and other chiefs' robes were beautifully worked with hair, beads, and jewels. His leggins were red, hand-somely worked with beads and horse-hair and ribbons, and his moccasins were fit for a prince to wear.

He has encountered the Utes, Pawnees, Snakes, Blackfeet, Crows, and Omahas. Thirty-three years ago, while he was the youngest of the braves, he engaged with a party of one hundred and twenty-five warriors of his tribe, and only twenty-five escaped alive. Twice was he wounded, and so distinguished by his daring that he was made a chief for his skill in fighting. Then he rose in rank to the highest station, and he holds it to-day. His people regard him as one of the greatest warriors on the plains, being skilled with the tomahawk, rifle, and bow and arrow, and in councils of chiefs, his wonderful sagacity and eloquence have stamped him, in the eyes of all Indians, as worthy of veneration and implicit obedience. As I had missed the party on their way to Washington by a few hours' tarrying on the "Chug," and General Smith had taken a short cut across to Pine Bluff Station, seventy-three miles below Cheyenne, to avoid a conflict anticipated about Richaud, I will give an account gleaned from others, of this expedition, which it is hoped may result in lasting peace.

The "outfit" assembled in front of General Flint's house, on their arrival at Fort Laramie, and got up a regular war-dance to amuse the general's family and others there. This chief, Red Cloud, whose fame had extended hardly east of the Missouri River, has now spread over the world; and from his wigwam and hunting-grounds, he is heard of across the Atlantic as a great man of destiny. He has passed through Omaha and Chicago to Washington in his war-paint, ornamented with eagle's feathers, buffalo-skins, horse-hair, bears' claws, and trophies of his skill, which he values more highly than a brigadier the stars upon his shoulders !

Along with him were nineteen of his braves and four squaws, which is a small number, considering that the Indian is a Mormon in the matter of polygamy. The Indian *buys* his wife (or wives) by giving a pony for the prize; and

1*

when Mother Bickerdyck, the army-nurse, saw "Friday" in Kansas, and upbraided him with having *two* squaws, he said, "Well, give me one white squaw, and I'll be content; you know one white squaw is equal to two Indian squaws!"

General Smith was a favorite of Red Cloud's, having met him in the Powder River country, and under circumstances which made him respected among the Sioux Indians.

The chiefs on Red Cloud's staff, and going to Washington, were:

Shem-ka-lu-tah, Red Dog.

Mon-tah-o-he-te-kah, Brave Bear.

Pah-gee, Little Bear.

Mon-tah-zia, Yellow Bear.

Makh-to-u-ta-kah, Sitting Bear.

Makh-to-ha-she-na, Bearskin.

Sha-ton-sa-pah, Black Hawk.

Shunk-mon-e-too-ha-ka, Long Wolf.

Me-wah-kohn, Sword.

Ko-ke-pah, Afraid.

Ke - cha - ksa - e - un - tah, The One that runs through.

Ke-yah-lu-tah, Red Fly.

En-ha-mah-to, Rock Bear.

Me-nah-to-ne-ow-jah, Living Bear.

Och-le-he-lu-tah, Red Shirt.

Squaws of High Blood.

Dah-sa-no-we, The White Cow Rattler, Sword's wife.

ISAAC H. TUTTLE, A CONVERTED INDIAN CHIEF.

INDIAN BOYS PRACTICING WITH BOW AND ARROW.

INDIAN BURIAL.

BISHOP CLARKSON CONFIRMING CONVERTED INDIANS IN
NEBRASKA AND DAKOTA.

GROUP OF CONVERTED INDIANS WITH THEIR PASTOR.

SPOTTED TAIL AND HIS SON.

Ny-ge-uh-ha, Thunder Skin, wife of Ke-cha-ksa-e-un-tah.

E-dah-zit-chu, The Woman without a Bow (Sansarc tribe), wife of Yellow Bear.

Mak-ko-cha-ny-un-tah-ker, The World Looker, wife of Black Hawk.

Along with them were John Richaud, the renegade, and a half-breed, James McCluskey. Also William G. Bullock, the post-trader at Fort Laramie, as familiar with the Indians as any one in those parts, unless it is a wealthy merchant in St. Louis, Mr. Beauvais, a Frenchman.

As the Indians entered the cars at Pine Bluff Station,—and one can hardly imagine what were their thoughts, because they had never before seen a train of cars or a locomotive,—a friend who was there said that, as soon as the cars started, the Indians expressed some terror in their countenances, and all at once grasped hold of the seats with both hands to hold on! As they passed through Columbus, on the road, several of the Pawnees (their deadly enemies) came in and shook hands with them. Arrived at Omaha, they were quartered at the Cozzens Hotel; but instead of occupying bedrooms and beds, they spread their blankets and skins on the floor, and sank down to a rest much coveted after a long and tedious journey of a thousand miles. Here crowds poured in from every quarter to interview these noted warriors; but as they did not speak English, they were only gazed at by curious people.

Red Dog ranks next as a warrior chief, and is much finer looking; but Man-afraid-of-his-Horses (sick at home) is head chief in civil matters.

Red Shirt is head chief of the White-Sash Band, of three hundred braves, is twenty-seven years of age, and was twice wounded in battle.

Long Wolf, with four ugly scars, is of the same band.

Black Hawk, wounded three times, is about second to Red Cloud as a bold warrior. All have distinguished themselves in various ways, and their buffalo-robes are worked and stained with figures and various objects, all of which tell the history of each one, describing minutely from childhood the first game they killed, whether a bird, antelope, or deer, and so on to some fight with an enemy,—all of which, clear as mud to me, is plain to them as a book. It is said that Red Cloud had prepared the following speech to make to his " Great Father," the President; but he changed his mind, and made another :

" Thousands of miles away, where the sun's last light falls on the big hills, I have left my people, to come and look my Father in the face. As that light makes us see all things around us clearly, so may the Great Spirit make our talk plain, that we may understand each other, and that our councils shall be as brothers who have met to smoke the pipe of peace. Father, I have heard that you are great and good. Listen to me, my Father, and let your ears hear one of your children, who comes from the wigwams of his people, with truth in his heart, and no lies upon his lips. I have made many treaties with your Commissioners, and they have promised many times, but have never kept their promises; and I have now come to see my Great Father myself, so that we can understand each other, and make no promises that we do not mean to keep. They have told you that I am a murderer; but I do not understand it in that way. You, Great Father, have driven me away from my country,—the only country I had to raise my children on. Tell me, Father, could any living man on this earth stand such a thing as this? Suppose I should go to your country, tear down your fences, and steal your cattle and your hogs, would you stand by and have no word to say? No, Father, I know you would not. In all the troubles of my people, the white man has been the first aggressor. Father, we are not cowards. We know that you are great, and that you can crush us with your mighty power. But we believe that you are good, and that you will protect your children, when they come to you for what they believe is theirs. We ask you to listen to us, to do by us as a good father should do by his children, and to let us carry back to our brothers and our people the assurance that the Great Spirit has smiled upon us, and that the Great Father is the Indian's friend, and the Indian's protector."

RED CLOUD'S JOURNEY.

The following piece of history is compiled from all that I could learn about a journey, which will be worth preserving, if only the results prove to be a lasting peace, as we hope and pray it will be.

In 1866, in searching for a short route to Montana and Idaho, the government took possession of the Powder River and Big Horn country, along the mountains, where gold is said to abound. A regiment of soldiers was ordered, under Colonel Carrington,—the 18th Regulars,—to open up a road and build forts for protection.

He went up by Fort Laramie, an old trading-post, situated on the North Platte River; from there he laid out one that shortened the distance from Omaha to Virginia City, Montana, three hundred miles. The colonel founded three forts, one on Powder River, one at the crossing of the Big Horn, and one on Tongue River. They were named Fort C. F. Smith, Fort Reno, and Fort Phil. Kearney,—after distinguished generals. These cost about six hundred thousand dollars. As soon as it reached the Indians that their country was to be occupied by the whites,

Red Cloud claimed the whole portion all along the Big Horn Mountains, and sent word to them that the Indians would kill all they met. Notice was sent to the government that if the soldiers did not withdraw north of the Platte, he would declare war. Of course no attention was paid to this, and the colonel went on to open roads, strengthen posts, and patrol the country. Some skirmishes took place between small bands of Indians and parties, but no fight of much account occurred till fall.

In October it was said that Red Cloud had given orders for all the Sioux to meet and prepare for war, and next month it was reported he was marching at the head of three thousand warriors. This the government as usual was slow to believe, and gave no heed to it. But early in December the Indians became troublesome along the Powder River country, and Red Cloud's policy was seen to guide them. The wily chief had planned the movement so as to strike a hard blow and capture Fort Kearney, and murder the garrison.

PHIL. KEARNEY MASSACRE.

Red Cloud collected all his warriors near the fort, and concealed them in the hills. Watching his opportunity, he surrounded and attacked a small party sent out against him from the post. As he expected, when the attack was made

known, the gates of the fort were thrown open,
and the main portion of the soldiers—cavalry
and infantry—marched out to rescue their friends,
corraled by the Indians. As soon as he got them
where he wanted, in the hills, he surrounded them
with his three thousand warriors, and cutting off
all chance of retreat, massacred every one of
them! So sudden was the surprise, that the
battle was over before a reinforcement could go
out, and the commander at once closed the gates
and remained in a state of siege, to protect those
who were not slaughtered. In the Phil. Kearney
massacre there fell three officers, forty-nine infantry, twenty-two cavalry, and two citizen em-
ployés, with Colonel Fetterman, the officer who
led them.

After the Phil. Kearney massacre, which
thrilled the country with horror, the government hastened to call a council with all the
tribes at Fort Laramie, and sent Generals Sherman, Harney, Sanborn, Terry, Augur, and Colonel Tappan to treat with them. Red Cloud kept
up his skirmishes and fights as occasion offered.
The 1st of August, 1867, the Sioux attacked and
killed Lieutenant Sternberg, of 27th Regiment
Infantry. And the next day quite a large body
of warriors engaged Major Powell and his soldiers
on the Piney Creek, four miles from Kearney, and
a severe battle was fought for hours. On the 27th,
some Indians came down—about one hundred

and twenty—to the hay-fields near the fort, and Lieutenant Belden, of 2d Cavalry (a good fighter), went for them with forty soldiers, and cleared them out. On the 3d November, Brevet Captain E. R. P. Shurley (whom the writer knew as post-adjutant in Camp Douglas, Illinois, and who was wounded in the war) was suddenly attacked on Goose Creek; he was desperately wounded, and his command was surrounded and " corraled" for some time, until troops came to his relief and saved the " outfit." Soon after, the train going to Phil. Kearney was attacked and corraled within three miles of the post. The 14th December, the wood-choppers for the forts were attacked on the Big Piney, and two men wounded. The forts now were in a state of siege, and communication between them became nearly cut off. The council at Laramie agreed to abandon that portion of the country, it being no longer needed, as freighting was changed to Montana, via Corinne, on the Pacific Railroad. But the Indians became impatient, and to hurry up matters, they kept on skirmishing from time to time. These were Sioux and some of the Arapahoes and Cheyennes.

In January, 1868, quite a *scare* was gotten up at Phil. Kearney by the sudden appearance of several hundred Sioux, Cheyennes, and Arapahoes, along with some friendly Crow Indians, and an attack was supposed to be meditated.

K

Dr. Matthews, one of the special peace commissioners, was there at the time, and he sent a message to the chiefs to meet him in council on the hill above the fort. Most of the Indians came, and after prayer by post-chaplain White, and a long smoke, the doctor made them a speech. After this, an old Sioux Indian, named the "Stabber," got up and said,—

"Whoever our father who has just spoken is, I believe he is a good man. We are told that the Great Father (President) sent word some time ago for his soldiers to leave the country, and I want to tell you that we want them to hurry and go. Send word to the Great Father to take away his warriors with the snow and he will please us. If they can go right away, let it be done, so that we can bring our old men, women, and children to live on these grounds in peace, as they did before you all came here. The Sioux, Arapahoes, and Cheyennes never fought each other until you came and drove away the game (meaning in the whole West), and then attempted to drive us away. Now we fight each other for sufficient ground to hunt upon, though all the lands to the east were once ours. We are talking to-day on our own grounds. God Almighty made this ground, and when He made it He made it for us. Look about you, and see how He has stocked it with game. The elk, the buffalo, and deer are our meat, and He put them here for us to feed upon. Your homes are in the East, and you have beef cattle to eat. Why, then, do you come here to bother us? What have you your soldiers here for, unless it is to fight and kill us? If you will go away to your homes and leave us, we will be at peace, but if you stay we will fight. We do not go to your homes, then why come to ours? You say we steal your cattle and horses; well, do you not know that when you come into our lands, and kill and drive away the game, you steal from us? That is the reason we steal your stock. I am done."

When "Stabber" sat down, "Black Hawk" (now *en route* for Washington) came forward and said,—

"Where was I made? I was raised in the West, not in the East. I was not raised in a chair, but grew upon the ground." He then sat down on the earth, and continued : " Here is my mother, and I will stay with her and protect her. Laramie has always been our place for talking, and I did not like to come here. You are getting too far west. You have killed many of our young men, and we have killed some of yours in return. I want to quit fighting to-day. I want you to take pity on us and go away."

A Cheyenne chief next addressed the council. He said,—

" We have been told that these forts are to be abandoned and the new road given up, and we have come over to see about it. If this is true, tell me so. I never thought we would come to a council so far west, but the old men prevailed and we are here. All last summer we heard that General Harney wanted to see us at Laramie, but we would not go. General Sherman also sent for us, but we would not listen while you were here. I do not know the name of my father there (pointing to Dr. Matthews), nor who at present is my Great Father (President) at Washington, but this I do know, my father (his parent) when he raised me told me to shake hands with the white man, and to try to live at peace with him, for he was very powerful. But my father also told me to fight my enemies, and since the white man has made himself an enemy I fight him. How are you our enemy? You come here and drive away our game, and he who does that steals away our bread, and becomes the Indian's bitterest enemy, for the Indian must have food to live. I have fought you, and I have stolen from you, but I have done both to live. The only road you have a right to travel is the Platte road. We have never crossed it to fight you. I am a soldier. I have a great many young men here who are soldiers, and will do my bidding. It is our duty to protect and feed our old men, women, and children, and we must do it. If you are friendly, why don't you give us powder and bullets to shoot game with? We will not use them against you, unless you do us harm. I want ten kegs, and when the other tribes know you have given them to me they will know we are good friends, and will come in and treat, and we will all live at peace. I come here to hear talk, not to make talk. We are poor. Take pity on us, and deal justly by us. I have done.''

The next speaker was a Crow chief, who, standing by the council-table, said,—

" Sioux, Cheyennes, Arapahoes, Crows, Father : I have been listening to your words, and they sound good. I hope you are not lying to each other. The Crows have long been the friends of the whites, and we want peace for all. We want powder, and when the white Father makes us presents, I want him to give us a good deal of ammunition."

An Arapahoe chief said :

"I want to say this: You are here with soldiers, and what for? Soldiers are your fighting men. Do you then want to fight? If so, tell us. If you desire peace, send your soldiers away. I have some of your stock. I would like to see you come and try to get it back."

This ended the talk on the part of the Indians, —then Dr. Matthews replied. He told them the Peace Commissioners would as willingly meet at Laramie as at any other place, but it was more convenient for the Indians to come to Fort Kearney. He did not promise them that the

к*   8

roads and country would be given up, or the posts abandoned. As to the powder the Indians asked for, he gave no reply, but said, " If the Indians cease fighting and keep the peace during the winter, the Commissioners will meet them in the spring and make a treaty, which will satisfy both them and us." The council broke up,—no good result being reached, —and the Indians being evidently in bad temper. When asked why Red Cloud did not come in to attend the council, a chief said, " He has sent us as the Great Father has sent you. When the Great Father comes, Red Cloud will be here !" This meant that the haughty chief would only treat through his agents, unless President Johnson came in person.

After the council in January, matters were unsettled all along the northwestern frontier until 10th April, 1868, when a large party of Indians appeared on the bluffs overlooking Phil. Kearney Fort. General John E. Smith (who was Red Cloud's choice to escort him to Washington) was at the time commanding the post, and made signals to the Indians to come in, but they refused to do so.

Most of the Indians carried scalp poles, and wore war-paint, to show that they were hostile. Finding that they would not come in, General Smith mounted his horse, and, taking an interpreter (Boyer), rode out to have a parley with them. The general wished to go up the hill, but the interpreter begged him not to do so, and then rode to the bottom and called out, " How ?" Then a chief replied, " How ?"

General Smith.—Come down, I want to talk.

Chief.—Who are you, and what do you want to talk about?

General Smith.—I am the chief at the fort, and want to see you.

Three Indians then advanced, and came slowly down the hill to where General Smith and Boyer were. When the chief, who was in his war-paint, came up, General Smith held out his hand, but the chief refused to take it, saying, " My brother was killed over there at the Phil. Kearney massacre, and I swore never again to shake hands with a white man."

General Smith.—Who are you, and who are those Indians on the hill ?

Chief.—I am a chief, and the warriors are part of Red Cloud's band. Here is his son (at the same time pointing to a young man who sat on a pony by his side).

General Smith.—What have you come here for ?

Chief.—We have been on the Laramie road, fighting the Snakes.

General Smith.—You were expected at the big talk at Laramie by the Peace Commissioners.

Chief.—I was there, and they promised that this country should be abandoned by your troops in two months. The two months are up, you are still here, and 1 see no sign of your moving.

General Smith (sharply). We have made some preparations to go, and will leave as soon as all is in readiness; but if your warriors commit depredations, or kill any more white men, we will not go at all, but stay here, kill you and drive off your game.

Chief (not noticing this threat). I want you to give me something to eat for my young men, and I will go over there and camp on the creek to-night.

General Smith.—I have nothing to give you, but I want to warn you to restrain your warriors from committing any depredations around here.

At this stage of the interview, a company of cavalry, which General Smith had ordered to saddle up and stand ready for any emergency, was seen filing out of the gates of the post, and as soon as the Indians caught sight of the troops, they whipped up their ponies and did not stop till out of sight.

General Smith was very much provoked at this interruption, by a stupid officer coming out when he had no business to do so,—and the impression of treachery on his part made on the minds of the Indians caused them to refuse to come back again to have another talk with him. Near sun-set, the Indians were seen crossing the plateau near the creek where the chief indicated he would camp. The evening gun fired as they crossed the stream, and the whole party halted and took a good look at the fort. After a confab among themselves, they seemed to think some sort of defiance had been shown them, and a warrior aiming his gun at the fort, fired. The ball struck on the parade-ground, but did no harm.

The Indians then went into camp, but went off next morning for Red Cloud's camp, which it is thought was not far off. General Smith soon after gave up the post, as ordered to from Washington; and in like manner Reno and C. F. Smith were abandoned, and the troops marched down to Fort Russell. The Indians did not attack the troops, but followed and stole stock when they could. No sooner were the forts abandoned than the Indians came in and set fire to the buildings, destroying property that cost the government over half a million dollars. They did this lest the troops should come back and occupy them again. But the giving up of these posts gave the Indians a false idea of their power, and they thought the government did it from fear.

Many of the Sioux now actually believe that their nation is more powerful than the United States, and Red Cloud a greater warrior than Grant, Sherman, or Sheridan. One of Red Cloud's party said, " If you are so strong and have so many warriors, why did you not keep

your forts on the Powder River?" The delegation to Washington will go back and tell the
people not how many men, women, and children
they saw, as evidence of our power and great-
ness, but how many horses, soldiers, guns, and
corn they saw. For thus they estimate the
power and glory of a nation.

Red Cloud won great glory among all the
Indians on the plains by his skill in manœu-
vring in getting us to give up four hundred miles
of rich territory, pulling down three forts, and
retiring back to the Platte River. No chief
since King Philip or Red Jacket has achieved
such a feat and a reputation as Red Cloud.

On account of repeated acts of hostility on the
part of the Sioux, the government refused to
trade with them at the posts, or have traders
sent among them. They need powder and lead,
etc., but it would be used to kill our people instead of game,—they allege it is needed, for now
it is more scarce.

Red Cloud came into Laramie and Fetterman
several times to get leave to trade, but at last he
said " he'd go to the Great Father at Washington,
and not treat with understrappers, with whom
he will in future have nothing to do." About the
middle of April he left his hunting-grounds, and
on the 24th appeared on the north bank of Platte,
opposite Fort Fetterman. With him were some
warriors, squaws, and children. They marched

down to the ferry in state, singing their song of welcome, and shouted across that they were in a hurry! They were halted there till next day, and the warriors allowed to come over unarmed.

Colonel Chambers, commanding, received them at headquarters. A long smoke all round followed, and then Red Cloud rose up and in a loud voice invoked the countenance and favor of the Great Spirit on his mission, shook hands with all the officers present, and went up to the council-table to have a long talk, as he had come a long way, and wanted to trade.

He said, " I have been treating with you since 1851, and no good has come of it. Our treaties do not last, and now I want to go and see the Great Father, and make a treaty that will last. Tell the Great Father I am here and desire to see him, and take fifty of my people with me to see him. I will wait for his reply at my camp beyond the river."

Colonel Chambers said he would "*blow the Great Father a message on his hollow wire*, and repeat all the chief had said to him," which quite pleased Red Cloud. He said, " I have waited for the soldiers to leave my country, and I want things settled."

The colonel intimated that the Father was at that time very far away at the East, and it might be many " sleeps" before he could hear from him, and as soon as the Father blew back words by the telegraph, he would send word to the chief's camp and let him know. He then asked to trade, and was allowed to buy tobacco and flour for robes left with the commissary, but nothing else.

He then spoke of his prisoner, John Richaud, and his wish to take him to Washington for a pardon. Also, that Riechaud had some property in the fort locked up, which he wanted a chief to take care of. Colonel C—— said he would not do that without orders from his chief (General Augur) at Omaha. This was satisfactory, and the chief sat down.

Speeches then were made by Man-afraid-of-his-Horses and Red Horse, and the council broke up.

Soon as it was known at Washington, and a consultation was had with General Sherman and Secretary of War Belknap, the President sent word that he would be glad to see the chief, and would send a guide to show him the way to the Great Father's wigwam. This message came the 12th May, and the Indians started on the 14th. A great dance was celebrated among the tribe of Ogallallas, and repeated at Fort Laramie for the officers and families.

To this point Red Cloud's son and wife came, but they returned with the others to their hunting-grounds in the Sioux country.

When the party under General Smith left the post in ambulances, etc., some felt "sea-sick," never having rode in a wagon before!

Once on the cars, it was kept as quiet as possible. At Frémont, forty-seven miles from Omaha, it had leaked out, and much excitement prevailed there, as it was reported that the Pawnees, the old and inveterate enemies of the Sioux, were coming in from their reservation (near there), and would attack the train and kill the Sioux chiefs. A number of them were there when the train came along, but they kept very quiet. One or two of the Pawnees went up and shook hands with their old enemies (with whom a deadly feud has existed for years), but they were closely watched by General Smith, lest a stab should be given with their knives. Although the Sioux chiefs were told of the danger, they were "as cool about it as a cucumber." They looked at their knives being all right, and that was all. Of course all along their route they were objects of curiosity to everybody ; and had the government declined to have them go (as it was said at first they would), a war would have followed soon after !

PERILOUS ADVENTURE—PURSUIT OF A HORSE-THIEF.

A young man named Frank Hunter, born in Massachusetts, migrated to the Indian country, and was very successfully employed as a government detective in " Camp Carling," between Cheyenne and Fort Russell. In the winter of

L

1868, a bold robbery was committed by a man employed in taking care of horses by Major J. D. Woolley, the post-trader at Fort Russell.

One morning in December the stable-door was left open, and soon found out that the man and two valuable horses were missing. One of them belonged to Lieutenant Wanless, of the 2d United States Cavalry (who was East at the time on leave); this was the fastest pacing horse in the territory, and for which he had refused a high price in money. The other belonged to the major, and was of considerable value. The matter of catching the thief and horses was given into Mr. Hunter's hands, with instructions to spare no pains or expense in securing the thief, who had hired out on purpose to steal the fast nag. The following I copied from the detective's journal, and verified the facts from other sources.

Mr. Hunter started out to Colorado with ten cavalrymen and Lieutenant Belden on the road to Denver *via* Boulder City, to prevent the thief (who went by the name of Durant) from getting into the mountains, and so on to New Mexico. This trip proved fruitless. The alternative that suggested itself was that the thief had gone another road, towards the Smoky-Hill route. The first tidings revealed the fact to them, at the South Platte River, that the inferior horse had been disposed of near Godfrey's ranch on the Platte, where the writer's horse and a beautiful

Cheyenne pony had been taken by horse-thieves
in the preceding summer. The thief, hard pushed
for money, had sold Mr. Woolley's horse to a
man here named Perkins, who paid thirty-five
dollars, while he was worth two hundred dollars.
This he placed out of the way, some thirty miles
off, thinking him safe from discovery.

Here the utmost caution and strategy were
necessary to recover this horse they had secreted,
and find out what road the rogues took with the
thoroughbred animal. But it was done. The
detective came back to Cheyenne with his escort
and left it there. Then, on one of Wells, Fargo
& Co.'s fast coaches, he embarked for Denver
City. A heavy snow-storm set in and impeded
the way. Thus the thief had nine days the start.

From Denver he made the best of his way—
after being detained five days by the storm—for
Sheridan, in Kansas, which was reached in five
more days' time,—the trip being made usually
by railroad in forty-eight hours. At Sheridan
the cars were blockaded with snow, and quite a
number of gentlemen were snow-bound, among
them the members of Congress from New Mexico
and Kansas. The detective proposed to these
honorable gents the pleasure of a tramp as far as
Fort Hays, only one hundred and thirty-five
miles! All agreed, and the party set out, though
the snow was very deep.

The expedition proved to be one of much interest; but the pursuit of the thief being the main object before us, we find the detective arrived at Fort Harker, Kansas, and in communication with a gentleman named Stone, who had seen the famous pacer, and had tried to buy him of the supposed owner; and from him the detective learned that the horse was near at hand, only twenty miles farther east, at a place called "Saline," on a small river, in Kansas. From this place the thief intended to convey the horse to Aurora, Illinois (his native town), to match him there with another, and thus to obtain a large sum of money for his thieving wickedness.

Arrived in Saline, Mr. Hunter lost no time in putting himself in communication with the sheriff there, who seemed to Mr. Hunter not to be entirely reliable; indeed, from a careful survey of faces of the loungers in the bar-room of the one-horse town of border settlers, the sheriff appeared to be hand-in-glove with the thief, so he concluded that his only chance of any help in the matter could come from the landlord and the telegraph operator,—the latter having sent messages from the rogue to Aurora, while detained there by the depth of snow. But no time was to be lost, and a desperate effort must be made.

Mr. Hunter went into the bar-room with the sheriff, after breakfast, and a crowd was sitting around the stove. The rogue was sent for with a message that "a gentleman wished to speak with him." He came into the room presently, picking his teeth, and putting on an assumed air of indifference; he looked at the detective with a coolness quite refreshing, as he stepped up to the bar and called for cigars, saying, " Gentlemen, who'll have a smoke ? I don't see any *gentleman* here that I know, besides myself."

" How are you, Ned ?" said Mr. Hunter. "You don't know me ?"

" Gentlemen," replied he, " on my honor, before God, I never saw this man before in my life! This is a put-up game of a man named Stone, to bilk me out of my fast horse ; and (putting his hand on his six-shooter in his belt) no man shall get this horse, which I bought, or me either, alive."

The detective with great presence of mind assured him that his game was up ; that the first motion he made of resistance he was a dead man ! Then drawing a pair of·manacles from his pocket, he soon clasped them on his prisoner's wrists, and relieved the rogue of his pistols, handing them over to the barkeeper for safety. He was taken to his room to pick up his traps, until the horse could be saddled up to return.

By this time a reaction had taken place among the crowd, who seemed to sympathize with the thief, and some exclaimed against taking him, and for all they knew, he might be innocent. Here was a new danger not expected. If these

L*

fifteen or twenty hard-looking customers should take it into their heads to vote the man guiltless, there was an end to justice, and the detective might find himself suspended from the nearest cottonwood limb of a tree, dangling like Mohammed's coffin, between heaven and earth! But as good luck would have it, the irons pressed tightly and painfully on the wrists of the captive, and he cried from his room, " Hunter! oh, Hunter! come and loose these cursed irons,—they're killing me !"

"Now, gentlemen," said Hunter, "you see whether he knows me or not." To the prisoner he said, " I'll loosen them if you'll tell all about it." He came in and said, " Yes, I stole the horse; I'm a thief, and that man is a detective of the government from Cheyenne."

Of course, here all danger should end, and my story cease. But the truth is, something new turned up very often to embarrass the journey back to Cheyenne. After leaving Fort Harker, a new dodge was attempted, but different from the one that Paddy essayed when he greased the horse's mouth to save the oats. Leaving the culprit in irons at Fort Harker, the detective proceeded on to Fort Ellsworth, Kansas, from which place he started in the morning with his horse, in high hopes of reaching Cheyenne in a few days.

But alas for the vanity of human hopes and

expectations! Having ridden about fifteen miles, the horse came to a sudden pause, and acted like one afflicted with spring-halt. Stopping at a ranch near by, after a careful examination, it was found that some precious villains had tied some silk cords on his legs underneath the fetlocks, thoroughly crippling him, so he could hardly move a limb. They hoped to lame the horse till he could be stolen again! But it was not successful. This journey of seventeen hundred miles cost the sum of six hundred dollars. But the horses were valued at fifteen hundred dollars, and it was right to put a stop, if possible, to the crime so common in the West of stealing horses, and one which subjects the culprit to a ball in his body, if needful to recapture stolen stock, and all say it is just and right, as a man's horse there may, in some cases, be " his life."

But the fellow while in limbo sawed off the chain and ball from his leg and escaped. He, moreover, had the impudence to write a saucy letter to Mr. Hunter, telling him " that the caged bird had flown, and the probability of their never meeting again !"

The rascal had been a soldier in the army, deserting several times, and re-enlisting under a new name each time, at different posts in the western country.

HANGING HORSE-THIEVES.

It seems awful when we hear of the "Vigilance committees" in new countries. They are a body of men combining together, in a secret society, to rid the community of vile men, who rob, steal, and commit murder, just as easy as lying, and all for a few dollars. I say it seems awful to hear of their sentencing individuals to be hung by the neck to the telegraph-poles, often with only a single hour's notice, without a trial by jury. But it is done in new towns such as Julesburg was, where people would not be safe without some such action. California began it, and other places found it necessary.

At Cheyenne, when it was full of these horse-thieves and gamblers, I was called upon to bury "a gentleman" (as he was called), who had died suddenly, they said, at the "Beauvais House." I went down from the fort in February, and as the day was pleasant, crówds of young men were gathered in front of the house, and the street was full of carriages. It seems the dead man was the proprietor of the hotel, and it did not bear a very good reputation. Harris had formerly a partner named Martin, with whom he had a quarrel one evening, and Harris ordered his former partner to leave,—shutting the door upon him. Then Martin turned and shot three balls through the panel of the door, one of which hit Harris, and of which he died in about twelve hours. This produced a great excitement, and called out the crowd at the funeral. The person in charge asked me to step out on the balcony and address the people in the street. But I declined, and said I would speak to the young men, as I felt it my duty to do, in the parlor and hall. I remarked to them " that the deceased was past our praise or blame. But it was my duty to warn them at this time, when no man's life was safe, to think of the shortness and uncertainty of human life! Here, away from good examples you once had at home, you are in much danger. You and I think that we will die on a sick-bed, with dear friends around us; but you nor I will die just when or where we expect to. Some of you *have learned to say your prayers at your mother's knee,* but you forget, or are ashamed to do so now. Oh, be warned, my friends, to seek Christ and his favor, and He will take care of you, etc."

I could see many faces intent on what I had to say, and among them was a little dwarf belonging to the house, as an errand-boy. He covered up his face with his hands, sitting upon a low stool, and perhaps his mind wandered back to the humble cottage where he was born, and a mother's smile was his best beacon of goodness: he had not forgotten ! For when I came back from the graveyard, he said, " Parson, I thought a good deal about what you said, indeed I did, *and it's true, every word of it, you bet!"*

Martin was tried by a court, and got clear. But he was fool enough to go round the saloons right away, boasting that he would serve out several more before breakfast. Then the vigilantes got hold of him that night, and hung him to the telegraph-poles near Cheyenne, till he was dead.

Sam Dugan was in our military prison at Fort Russell, for the crime of stealing horses. He was released upon a writ of *habeas corpus* from Colorado and taken to Denver, where members of the vigilance committee took him from jail outside the city in an express-wagon, and fastening a rope around his neck, and throwing it over a limb of a large cottonwood-tree, they hung him up; leaving the body suspended for twenty-four hours.

He confessed to have stolen many horses, and to have murdered at least six men in his life on the plains.

Most of these hardened villains die as brave men; but Dugan they said whined like a child. He was really afraid to die, because of his great wickedness.

AN INDIAN FIGHT AT SWEETWATER MINES.

On the morning of the 4th May, 1870, there was a desperate fight with two companies of the 2d United States Cavalry, under Major D. S. Gordon and Lieutenant C. B. Stambaugh, a god-child of General Sherman. The Indians had committed some outrages, in return for which a party of miners killed a chief named Black Bear, his squaw, and eleven other Indians, Arapahoes.

When the principal chief of the Arapahoes heard of the fate of Black Bear and his party, he was very angry, and called together three hundred warriors (the tribe only numbering about fifteen hundred souls), and marched for Atlantic City, as it is called (a small town in the Wind River valley). Two companies of cavalry camped near the place just before the Arapahoe warriors appeared. A young man named Bennett saw them first, as he was driving his mules from the pasture. The Indians at once sur-rounded him and marched for the town, to kill him in sight of the village, where the troops were, but not known to the Indians. Bennett soon saw they were taking him towards a gulch close by the village where Gordon and Stambaugh were camped.

On coming up to the top of the hill, the camp

was in full view, and only a few hundred yards away.

Bennett shouted at once for help, and, putting out as hard as he could, soon got into camp safe and sound. The sight of the military astonished the Indians so that they did not try to recapture Bennett, but made good time in every direction to escape. The soldiers were just getting up for "*reveille*," when the guard saw Bennett coming with the Indians, they driving and whipping him with their bows. The shout rang out, "Indians! Indians!" and at once they opened fire, officers and soldiers tumbling out of their beds. Some had on their drawers only,—some in one stocking, and many without boots,—all seized their arms, and rushing to the picket lines, unhitched their horses, jumped on with no time to saddle, and without hats galloped over the hills in pursuit of the flying Indians. Learning that some cattle were run off near the town, some of the soldiers galloped through the streets and hallooing "Indians!"—a cry the most terrible of all alarms along the border,—soon brought every man to his feet, and gun in hand, rush out to meet the foe. Soon these half-naked warriors had cleared the hills of the red men, and strolling home as the sun rose over the bluffs, when a horseman came into Major Gordon's camp with the news that "Miner's Delight" camp was attacked, and the teams of Mr. Fleming, who was hauling hay for the government. Major Gordon taking Lieutenant Stambaugh, Sergeant Brown, and nine privates (all the soldiers in the camp), and leaving orders for the rest to follow as fast as they came in, they set off for the hay-field, distant about eight miles. There they saw none, as the Indians had left, but striking their trail, went on as fast as possible. A storm had been gathering all the morning, and soon as they had gone six miles, it burst upon them with terrible fury, completely covering up all traces of the enemy. The major thinking it useless to follow further, set out to return to the post; but he had not gone far before he encountered a lot of about sixty Indians. The snow and sleet was so blinding at the time, that he did not see them until he came close upon them. A charge at once was ordered, and the troops dashed forward, scattering the Indians in every direction. Unfortunately, however, in the attack Lieutenant Stambaugh received a ball from an Indian's pistol, and Sergeant Brown had his jaw broken by another shot. Lieutenant S——, though wounded, was held on to his horse by Major Gordon, until surrounded by an immense crowd of desperate warriors, when Gordon told Stambaugh, " For God's sake, hold on to the mane of your horse, as I have to shoot!"

Lieutenant S—— fell off soon after, valiantly fighting. He was shot through the head side-

M

ways,—from the throat up through his brain,—
through the chest, arms, and hands. He was
brave to a fault, and the Indians probably
took him for a "brave" white chief of high
rank.

Seeing these two men fall from their horses,
and that few soldiers were there, the Indians
rallied and charged them furiously. A severe
fight followed over the body of Stambaugh, the
savages trying to capture and scalp it, and the
soldiers defending it nobly. Six Indians were
killed and two soldiers wounded. Soon the
Indians retreated, leaving their wounded and
dead with the soldiers. The fight lasted about
two hours. All then became quiet, and Major
Gordon descended the ridge,—a strong position,
—and carrying the body of Stambaugh a piece,
hid it away in some bushes. Expecting the
Indians would attack him on the way, he set out
for camp, the Indians having gone that way. He
saw no more of them, however. Late at night
with his men he reached Atlantic City, they
having eaten nothing since the day before.

Strange it was, the reinforcements he had ordered did not reach him, and none knew where
they were. Of course all the miners there were
greatly excited; the events of the day were talked
over, rockets thrown up, and fires kept burning
on the hills as beacons for a guide to the soldiers
still out; but before daylight they all came in,

after having lost their way in the storm while searching for Major Gordon and his party.

Early next morning, Lieutenant Dinwiddie took a strong detachment of troops and twenty citizens and went out to the scene of battle, and taking up the body of young Stambaugh, marched slowly back on their sad journey with the noble brave fellow to the camp, which should know him no more!

INDIAN ATTACK ON THE STAGE-COACH GOING TO DENVER—REV. MR. FULLER'S ACCOUNT OF TWO ATTEMPTS UPON HIS LIFE.

The following letter tells its own story. Moreover, it is a truthful narrative, and shows to the young that a Christian man is a bold man to meet danger, knowing that God helps us, while we use all proper means of safety to help ourselves.

PITTSBURG, May 30th, 1870.

REV. E. B. TUTTLE, Cheyenne, Wyoming Ter.

REV. AND DEAR SIR,—I will try to give you a brief account of my adventure with the Indians, in answer to your request. It was on the 1st day of June, 1867, the same year that the Right Reverend Bishop Tuttle went out to his jurisdiction (whom I met a few days after the adventure at the North Platte Station). The scene of the adventure was Fairview Station, which was a deserted ranch about ten miles east of "Fort

Wicked," or Godfrey's ranch. The station house had been burned, and the high adobe walls with an open front entrance, facing the road, were left standing. About half-past two P.M. we stopped at " Godfrey's" for a change of horses and re- freshments. I was the only passenger, and as we started on, the company consisted of the driver, myself inside the coach, and two horsemen, " stock leaders" (employed by the stage company to transfer stock from one point to another), four in all. Unsuspectingly, we went straight into the Indian's trap. It was about four P.M. I sat on the front seat with my back to the driver, the windows being down. The first thing that caught my attention was the discharge of a number of rifles, some of the balls crashing through the sides of the coach.

The Indians were well armed with rifles, bows and arrows, and were all mounted. Instantly I seized my revolver (a small six-shooter), and made ready to defend myself. I saw the two horsemen wheel their horses and start back towards " Godfrey's" Station. They were just a little behind the coach. The driver also yelled at his horses and gave them a short turn, for the same purpose, no doubt. While we were turn- ing round, a tall Indian rode up close to the coach-window and looked in, and as he did so I looked out; our faces met only about six feet apart. He had a rifle in one hand; I saw him

drop his rein and grasp his gun with both hands.
I heard the click of the trigger. I could easily
have shot him, having my revolver in my hand,
but I did not,—why I do not know. It was well
that I did not, as it proved. I dropped under the
coach-window to avoid his fire, if possible. He
fired and rode on quickly ahead, his shot being
delivered either at the driver or myself, I know
not which. The horses and coach were now
turned about and faced towards " Godfrey's,"
and were running as only thoroughly frightened
horses will run. They were large, powerful
animals, four in number. The Indians had meantime divided themselves into two bodies. (There
were about thirty of them in all, of the Cheyenne tribe. I will shortly state how they were
numbered.) One party starting in pursuit of the
horsemen, and the other remaining with the
coach to take it.

The situation was most critical. I soon saw
that the horses did not keep the road, but turned
out of it towards the Platte River (the river and
the road run parallel about half a mile apart,
as you probably know), and I knew that the
driver was not guiding them! Putting my revolver
in my side-pocket, I opened the door and, taking
hold of the railing above, looked first to see if
the driver was indeed gone. He was not there!
I did not turn back; to stay inside was sure death.
If there was any chance of escape, it was from

M*

the outside. I sprang out to the driver's seat above, but judge of my dismay to find the *reins on the ground!* I intended to get control of them. I knew not what to do, but had an idea at first of jumping to the ground to get the reins. While standing there thinking how to manage to get the reins, I was the only mark for the Indians, and was fired at a number of times. Such was the situation, standing alone on the coach-box,—the Indians before and behind endeavoring to shoot me and to stop the coach,—and yet I escaped. I have yet the coat, with a bullet-hole in the sleeve, which I had on. My escape was in this wise : I saw that the reins might be reached from the headstalls of the wheel-horses. I therefore sprang down on to the tongue of the coach to get them, but just then the horses had reached a slough about two rods wide and as many feet deep, with a sharp bank on either side. They did not stop, but plunged into and across it. I fell fortunately over the nigh horse's back, just clearing the wheels. The horses and coach went on and I was left in the slough. That fall to me at the time appeared sure death. I expected to be killed instantly. But, sooner than I can tell it, I was upon my feet upon the bank, my revolver in my hand, determined not to be taken alive; for well enough I knew what that would end in. To my astonishment, the Indians did not stop to give me a shot even; being under a full run, they barely glanced at me as they passed in pursuit of the coach. I saw the reason of this. I was on foot, and between me and "Godfrey's" was another body of Indians. They were all mounted and armed; I could not run away; I was in a vice apparently.

I looked towards the river, and observing some islands in it, my plan was instantly formed. If I could only reach the river, I would swim out and get behind one of the islands. And the river being high and turbid, with a quicksand bottom, I did not believe they would venture to come after me. (I had learned to swim when a boy, and that now was my means of salvation.) I started for the river as soon as the last Indian had passed me, "double quick," but as I started, I glanced towards the west, and, to my dismay, saw the other party coming back at a distance of four or five hundred rods from me, and I had at least two hundred rods to make to reach the river. They had got through with their chase of the two men. They had killed one of them and also his horse (I buried his body the next day). The other man being mounted on a trained racer, as I afterwards learned, managed by hard running to escape and reach the station.

At a certain angle bearing back towards "Godfrey's," I started for the river, and the Indians turned to run in between me and the river.

But Providence interposed again. Within one minute from the time of my fall, the Indians stopped the coach, shooting one of the horses to do it; and this drew the attention of the other party away from me to the coach, being drawn (I suppose) by motives of plunder on seeing the coach stopped. I have since learned that they do not divide the plunder in any civilized way, but what an Indian gets his hands on is his. But for this circumstance, they must have got between me and the river. Finding that I had actually gained the river-bank, I determined not to go in at once, but the rather to get as far away as possible, while the Indians were engaged in plundering the coach, knowing it would take them some minutes to do that. I had no hope of running away, but slipping off my boots, I began a rapid walk up the river-bank, all the while glancing back at the Indians, expecting momentarily that they would start for me. Thus I got nearly a mile away, when I noticed two men in the road, a little ahead of me. I stopped as soon as I saw them, feeling sure that they were Indians who had been sent to that point to prevent my escape. As I stopped, they made signs for me to come to them; but this I took to be a decoy, under a pretense of friendship, to get me away from the river. Instantly divesting myself of my outer clothing, I plunged in, see-ing them start for me as I did so, at a full run.

There were no islands there, and to get away, I must make the other side. The water was very cold, the current strong, and I soon became chilled. I found my strength going fast, and gave up my last hope of escape. I would have gone under but for another interposition of Providence. I drifted on to a *sand bar*, and stopping there, I expected to die. I did not wait long. In a brief time the two men had reached the river-bank opposite me, and judge of my joy, dear sir, to see the uniform of United States cavalry soldiers!

They had been sent out (from Fort Morgan) two days previous to search for some deserters. They happened to come upon the ground just then, else I should not be writing you this account to-day. They saw the whole affray from the outset, but did not dare to attack. They counted the Indians and said there were about thirty of them. Now, when I started for the river, after the fall, they agreed to assist me if they could. Fortunately I did not go in immediately on reaching the river, but went towards them without knowing of their presence. When I went into the river finally, they understood that I mistook them for Indians, and made a dash to save me. God bless them! In doing that they put themselves in danger. I saw this and spoke of it, but they said they intended to give the "red devils" to understand thus that they were supported by others. Their strategy had precisely that effect. I looked towards the Indians, and they were making off in the other direction towards "the bluffs," as fast as they could go. We went safely back to " Godfrey's," one of the soldiers kindly giving me his horse to ride. I wish it were in my power to reward in some substantial way these noble young men. After saluting me from the river-bank, I swam and waded back to the shore. It was with diffi-culty that I could stand when I reached it. My coat was stained with patches of blood. The soldiers at first were sure that I was wounded, but strange to say, I was not hurt. The blood was from the driver, and got upon my coat from the coach-box.

I lost my baggage, several hundred dollars of goods and money captured by the Indians. Stopping two days at " Godfrey's," with a force of eighteen men well armed, in three coaches bound east, we started on again. Godfrey, who has a mortal hatred of Indians, treated me with great kindness. This, dear sir, was my marvel-ous escape. Bishop Randall writing me after-wards about it, said, that it seemed to him but little short of a miracle. Bishop Tuttle also ex-pressed the same view. The fall from the tongue of the coach, the stopping of the coach just in time to call off the party that were getting be-tween me and the river, the sand bar in the river, on which I rested in the last extreme, and finally, the singular appearance of the soldiers to deliver me, are plain indications that it was the will of God that I should be spared.

Truly yours,

Wm. A. Fuller.

CHAPLAIN WHITE SAYS THERE'S A TIME TO PRAY
AND A TIME TO FIGHT.

In July of the same year as the massacre at Phil. Kearney, that is to say on the 20th July, while Chaplain White was traveling on Powder River with Captain Templeton, Lieutenant Daniels, Lieutenant Wanns, and J. H. Bradley, in company with five white women and two colored also, going to join their command, and while quietly traveling along, about fifty to sixty wild Indians came suddenly upon them just as they approached " Crazy Woman's Fork River." At once there was a panic, and one of the officers suddenly put on a woman's bonnet and rode off. One woman had a babe. The chaplain, seeing all was confusion, and each one for himself, exclaimed, " For God's sake, don't leave these women to be murdered!" This seemed to call them to their senses, and they began to rally, though, all told, there were but thirteen armed men. One soldier, a German, got terribly frightened, and said, "*Isn't there some one to pray ?*" The chaplain seized him by the collar and bid him hold his gun, saying, " *There is a time to pray and a time to fight!*" By nightfall they had all disappeared. Lieutenant Bradley was very courageous; for when the Indians shot their arrows, he would stoop down and pick them up in derision.

Chaplains may be sometimes of little account, but if their record could be written up, a large number would be found to have done noble service during the war of the rebellion.

Chaplain John McNamara, of the 1st Wisconsin Regiment, was one of them. I learned the following anecdote from a soldier who died in Camp Douglas:

Private Auchmuty said, " We had marched for a whole year, and had never a battle. Like all soldiers, we grumbled a good deal, and found fault with our rations. Our chaplain preached a sermon about our being discontented, saying we ' had done nothing at all for the government, only to soldier a little, and eat our rations.' This made us a little angry, and so we took it out in calling as he passed, '*There goes the chaplain that eats his rations!*'

" But by-and-by we had a sharp and bloody fight at Stone River. Colonel B. J. Sweet was badly wounded in his right arm, and our captain was killed. This made us waver and fall back. But the chaplain rushed forward to lead us, exclaiming, ' Boys, come on ! The enemy is wavering; we are sure of a victory!' On we rushed after him, and drove the foe off the field. After that we called him the 'Bully chaplain.' He lost his wig, but he gained the victory."

LEGEND OF "CRAZY WOMAN'S FORK."

The Absarakas, or Crow nation, have the reputation of being good friends to the whites, and it is also said they have never warred with them.

Iron Bull, a renowned chief of the Crows, relates the following legend.

In the journey through that most delightful region of Montana from Fort Phil. Kearney to Fort C. F. Smith (in the Powder River country), one of the most favored camping-grounds is the one called "Crazy Woman's Fork," the name of a pretty little stream of water that rises in the Big Horn Mountains, and emptying into the Little Horn River. About three miles from the mountains this stream crosses the trail between the two military posts mentioned.

This camp on the Fork is noted for its danger from Indian attacks, as an abundant supply of game being found in the valley, brings the Indian there to replenish his larder of wild meat. Notwithstanding the dangers attending a journey through this region, it has its attractions in the beautiful and diversified views of lovely

N   10

scenery, which hasten the parties traveling that region to encamp, for a night at least, on the banks of a limpid stream that refreshes man and beast from an unfailing source in the mountains. The banks are skirted with cottonwood-trees, and to the west, one sees the tall spurs of the Rocky Mountains rising up, as it were, from your feet, their dizzy heights covered with snow; while the haze that surrounds them gives to them a halo of glory and weirdlike appearance, that the im- aginative might compare to *the garments that mantle the spirits of the blessed in Paradise!*

Iron Bull said that about two hundred years ago, when the moon shone brighter, and there were more stars, his nation was a great people, and they roamed over all that country from the Missouri River to the west of the Yellowstone, and no dog of a Sioux dare show himself there. But the people had been wicked, and the Great Spirit had darkened the heavens and made the sun to shine with such heat that the streams were dried up, and the snow disappeared from the highest peaks of the mountains. The buffalo, the elk, the mountain sheep, the deer, and the rabbit, all disappeared and died away, bringing a great famine upon his tribe, and the spirit of the air breathed death into the lodges, so that the warrior saw his squaw and papooses die for want of the food he could not find on all the plain, or on the mountain-sides; so that the whole nation grieved and mourned in sorrow of heart.

Still, they kept up their wars with the Sioux, and fought many a bloody battle with them when they suffered most, and the game had entirely disappeared. Their great medicine-man called a council, and when the head-men had assembled, he told them of a wonderful dream that he had had, when he was bidden by the Great Spirit to gather the chiefs of the tribe at the fork of the stream where they lived.

Their ponies had all been eaten for food, so the proud Indians were compelled to make the journey on foot to the place of meeting.

But when they had arrived at the bluffs, on the edge of the valley, they were surprised to see a bountiful supper spread on the bank of the stream, close by the Forks, and a white woman close by, standing up and making signs to them to descend from the bluffs.

Having never before seen a " white squaw," they were greatly astonished. The medicine-man descended to the valley. The white woman told him that the Great Spirit would talk to the council through her. She told him that the wars of the tribe were displeasing to the Great Spirit, and they must make peace with the Sioux nation. When that was done, the great chief, " The-Bear-that-grabs," must return to her.

They sent out runners to the Sioux, and peace

148

was declared between the tribes for the first time in one hundred years.

She then told the great chief to follow the mountain in a westerly course, until he came to the Big Horn River, and where the rock was perpendicular, *he was to shoot three arrows, hitting the rock each time.*

The chief departed on his mission, and as he gained the bluffs from the stream, he looked back at the white squaw, but what was his surprise when he saw her rising in the air and floating towards the mountains! He watched her until she disappeared over the highest peak towards the sky.

The chief pursued his journey, and, arriving at the place told him by the white squaw, he discharged his arrows. The first one struck in rock. The second flew over the mountain. The third was discharged, and a terrible noise followed: the heavens were aglow with lightning; the thunder shook the mountains. The earth trembled, and the rocks were rent asunder, and out of the fissure countless herds of buffalo came, filling the valleys and the hills. The hearts of the Indians were glad, and they ate and were merry, and returned thanks to the Great Spirit and to the good white woman.

The great fissure in the rocks is the cañon of the Big Horn River.

Iron Bull avers that when anything of note is

about to befall the tribe, the image of the white woman can be seen hovering over the peak of the mountain at " Crazy Woman's Fork." He says the Crows have never killed any of the whites, and his people say and believe " that they are treated by the government agents worse than the tribes who give us all the trouble."

In other words, because they are peaceable, we need not, as with others, to buy them off with presents. And they say we have taken some of their lands and given them to the Sioux, who were fighting and destroying the whites as often as they could.

PHIL. KEARNEY MASSACRE.

One of the most fearful and fatal massacres on the plains that is known, occurred in the forenoon of December 21st, 1866, at Fort Phil. Kearney, Dakota.

About nine o'clock, some Indians, a few only (as usual), were seen on the bluffs. Brevet General Carrington, Colonel of the 18th United States Infantry, in command of the post, sent out eighty-one men, one company of infantry, and one of 2d Cavalry, Company C, under command of Colonel Fetterman. The instructions, it is said, were not to go over the hills. However that may be, they pursued the hostile Indians beyond sight of the post, crossing the river near the fort to do so. At ten o'clock the fight be-

N*

gan, the firing being heard plainly at the post.
There were from fifteen hundred to twenty-five
hundred Sioux, under chief Red Leaf.

The soldiers were led into an ambuscade, and
having shot away all their ammunition in a
panic, were surrounded and massacred before
two o'clock in the afternoon. Sixteen Indians
were killed, and chief Spider among them. The
bodies of the soldiers were horribly mutilated
and scalped. Why reinforcements were not sent
out to help them out of their perilous condition
does not appear. Colonel Fetterman was killed,
a noble, brave man, and the fort next above
"Laramie" was named after him. This is an
eyesore to Red Cloud, and he requested the
President to have it removed, as of no use, he
said, and costing the government a great deal of
money. His wish was not gratified.

MAUVAISES TERRES, OR BAD LANDS, DAKOTA.

Up in the Indian country, in Dakota, near White
River, as one travels over a prairie country, one
comes suddenly upon a valley, down between
one and two hundred feet, which is at least
thirty miles wide, by ninety in length. It looks
as though it had sunk down below all the country
round; while standing like sentinels all around,
one sees pillars of immense height, of irregular
prismatic columns of masses of stone, stretching

up tò the height of from one to two hundred feet or more. It reminds one of the ruins of Pompeii (described by Bulwer) as the traveler wends his way through deep passages, amidst petrified snakes, turtles, and mammoth animals, which must have been larger than elephants. Turtles weighing a thousand pounds, petrified, lie around, and all over is strewn the remains of extinct animals in this vast charnel-house.

Professor Leidy, of· Philadelphia, has detected about thirty remains of species of extinct mammalia. Many of these belonged to animals such as the hippopotamus, rhinoceros, tapir, etc. One extinct animal, called the Oreodon, had grinding teeth like lions, cats, etc., and must have belonged to a race that lived on vegetables and flesh, and yet chewed the cud like a cow. Another called the Machairodus, was wholly carnivorous, and combined the size and weight of the grizzly bear with the jaws and teeth of the Bengal tiger. Most of the bones are yet in good preservation and highly mineralized. Dr. Owen says he saw all the bones of a skeleton eighteen feet long and nine in height; also a jaw of a similar animal, which measured five feet along the range of its teeth. At one place there is a valley which has the appearance of a floor of an ancient lake, where turtles lie imbedded by hundreds, and some weighing a ton. This wonderful place looks like the city of the dead ; and as nothing grows there, and there is no water for animals, no living thing is found there, not even a bird. General Sully made a forced march through it with cavalry a few years ago, and had to carry water for the men and horses. The Indians never go there, unless driven in by some tribe attacking in superior numbers. The fossils which have been brought from the Mauvaises Terres belong to a species that became extinct before the period when the Mastodon inhabited this country. The strata in which these animals are imbedded indicate that the water was fresh or brackish. It is the most desolate and barren prospect one could lay his eyes on ; and if the place for bad people is like this, when they come to die, may no boy have to go there and be frightened all his life-long for his wicked and cruel deeds to others, or to animals either ; for the sight of these skeletons is enough to make any boy afraid of disobeying his mother, or to go to sleep any night without being sorry for his sins.

Gold is said to be deposited there, and may yet be found in large quantities, if the Indians can be induced to let the whites prospect there. Awhile since, an Indian brought into a fort some gold-dust and a large nugget. The post-trader looked at it and pretended it was iron, saying to the Indian, " No good." He threw it out of the window and gave the Indian a glass of

whisky. When he went out, the tradei picked
it up, and it was worth thirty dollars. The Indian
having refused to tell where he got it, was made
quite drunk, and then he said it came from the
Bad Lands; but if the chief found out he had
told of it, he would kill him.

NATURAL HISTORY—ANIMALS ON THE PLAINS.

The animals which are found west of the Missouri River, especially in the Rocky Mountains,
and far beyond them, are the buffalo, elk, deer,
cimarron bear, mountain sheep, antelope, coyote, prairie-dog, etc.

The buffalo, which affords good beef to the
Indian hunters, and has fed many thousand
toilers over the plains to Salt Lake and California, is mainly known to boys in the comfortable buffalo robes, which every one knows the
use of in sleigh-riding. But to us officers and
soldiers on the plains they are life-preservers
almost, in our sleeping out nights on the ground,
far away from home and good beds and blankets.

The buffalo meat is tough, unless from a young
cow; and the Indians make little difference in
drying it for winter use, as they have good teeth
and always a first-rate appetite. The skins are
dried and tanned by the squaws, who lay them
on the grass; and I saw an old gray-haired squaw
toiling away with a sharp instrument, made of

the end of a gun-barrel, something like a carpen-
ter's gouge, and this had a bone handle, with which
she kept scraping off the inside of the skin of its
fibres, so as to make it soft and pliable. She had a
stone to sharpen the tool with, and as she leaned
over, tugging away, the perspiration rolled off her
face in streams. Poor old creature, I felt sorry for
her, as the work might have been done by several
big, lazy, half-grown Indian boys I saw romping
around and shooting their arrows at a mark.
But it is disgraceful for the *lords of creation to
labor*, so they only kill the game, and leave the
squaws to cure and prepare it for eating.

It is astonishing how poorly Indians are com-
pensated for their robes and furs. In Colorado,
some Indians had been very successful in killing
buffaloes, had plenty of meat, and purchased with
their robes flour, sugar, coffee, dry-goods, and
trinkets from the white and Mexican traders; but
they did not realize one-fourth their value. They
were worth eight or nine dollars by the bale at
wholesale. The traders paid seventy-five cents in
brass wire or other trinkets for a robe; two dollars in groceries, and less in goods. Six tribes,
in 1864, furnished at least fifteen thousand robes,
which, at eight dollars, would amount to one
hundred and twenty thousand dollars. The
traders literally swindled the poor Indians. *They
will give the robe off their backs for a bottle of whisky
on the coldest day.*

The cimarron bear is avoided by the soldiers, if possible, when met by them. Up in the Wind River country, a soldier was mauled terribly by one which he had wounded, but failed to kill cn the first fire. The fight was desperate, for the bear, said to have been six or seven feet long, and weighing nine hundred pounds, had clinched the soldier, and both rolled down the ravine together, the other soldiers afraid to fire lest they should hit the poor comrade, almost in the jaws of death. They did rescue him, however, by lunging a knife into bruin's side, compelling him to release his hold, after lacerating the soldier's arm and side.

The coyote is a kind of wolf that preys on the antelope. It is a mean, sneaking thief, too mean to attack a herd of antelopes, but follows them up, and while one strays off, grazing, watches the opportunity to spring upon his victim, run him down, and snap the hamstring of poor antelope, and then eats him.

One night I was woke up at Fort Sedgwick, thinking I heard wild geese flying over. But I learned it was a drove of coyotes, which came over the bluffs, into and through the fort nightly, to eat the refuse meat outside, where beef was slaughtered. They prowl about, and sometimes make a noise like a lot of school-children halloo-ing at play. They never bite, unless attacked. An old lady got lost about a mile outside the post, at Russell, in the winter. She started out of Cheyenne, one Monday afternoon, to search for an emigrant train which might be going to Montana, where she had a son living.

She strayed away and was found in a snowbank, by some soldiers going out to dig a grave. She was glad to see the faces of white men, for it was on Friday, and she had thus been out, wandering around since Monday, four days! She was brought into the hospital and given a warm cup of tea. "Dear me," she exclaimed, "give me a quart,—I'm almost famished!" She said she was only frightened by the coyotes coming round nights and barking at her. Her feet were partly frozen, but in a few weeks she went on to Montana.

The black-tailed deer are fine eating; the grass on which they feed in the mountains is said to make the meat tender and sweet.

The mountain sheep are large and very strong; they will throw themselves from a rocky cliff and strike on their head many feet below unharmed, being protected by horns and stout necks. They are larger than our domestic sheep.

The antelope is a pretty, gazelle-like creature, fleet and agile in springing up and running. Having passed over the Union Pacific Railroad many times, it has been my pleasure to see them running away from the train in droves of a dozen or more, in file one after the other, till out of sight, far away over the bluffs. By-and-by they will disappear as the buffalo have, driven away by approaching civilization. The young are easily caught and tamed, and make nice pets for children. The cost of one here is usually five dollars. They are hunted a good deal for their meat, as antelopes are tender and sweet to the palate. One method in hunting them is to raise a white or red flag, and the silly creatures, full of curiosity, will turn and walk towards it till shot down by the marksman.

The prairie-dog is an animal peculiar to the plains. He is found in what is called a " dog-town ;" being a plot of a few acres, as seen along-side the railroad, after a day and night's ride, dotted over with mounds a foot or so high. Sometimes a thousand or more congregate in the town, and their holes are a few rods apart. When approaching these towns, or the cars pass along, you see them scamper off to the top of the mound, stand up on their hind-legs and bark, shaking their little short tails at each bark, and presently plunge head first into their holes. They are of a brown color, size of a squirrel, but with tails an inch long. I tried to drown out some, and poured several barrels of water into a hole without bringing any out. These holes ramify into others, generally, so it was im-possible, in my experience, though others do get hold of a single hole, and drown them out.

o

Rattlesnakes and small owls make their homes
with them. These are interlopers, as the prairie-
dogs dig the holes down about three to four feet.
They can be tamed, as I know by experience,
having carried several east to Chicago, to my
Sunday-school children.

One night in Colorado, on the Cache le Poudre
River, while camping out there (having gone with
a detective in search of horse-thieves), I heard a
terrible clatter among the prairie-dogs late in the
night. It was explained to me by the ranch-
man, who said they were in the habit of chang-
ing their domiciles once a year, and it was only
effected after a great struggle and fight among
themselves. By sunrise, four o'clock in the
morning, all was still; and the little fellows were
running about in search of roots, upon which they
live all winter, down in their dark, deep holes.
They belong to the species marmot, and are said
to be good eating. I have never tried them.
Friday, Arapahoe chief, told me that the Indians
make use of their oil to cure rheumatism.

A NIGHT SCENE.

The Bishop of Nebraska visited the Pawnee
reservation, near Columbus, and the head chief
had just before lost his only son by death. He
was feeling very unhappy about it, and he told

the interpreter to say to "The little medicine-man-in-the-big-heap-sleeves," " That he had lost his son, and was feeling very heavy here" (lay-ing his hand upon his heart); adding, " All is dark, and I want him to tell me what the Great Spirit has got to say to me in my sorrow."

The bishop said, "Tell him that we have a prayer in the book, we always say, 'for persons in afflic-tion;' we will all kneel down and repeat it sen-tence by sentence, and remain in silent prayer." There in the shadows of the evening, a few whites mingling among the dusky faces, as the lights shone upon their bent forms, prayer was offered for consolation and healing of the poor old man's heart. It was a solemn scene, and many sobs were heard from the Indian women. After a little while, all rose up from their knees, and the tall chief, standing erect, said, with beam-ing eye, "Say to the Father, say to him, it's all gone! all gone!" He added, " We are glad to hear such words from the Great Spirit. We have been told many words from our fathers many moons since; they have told us good words; that when we do wrong the Great Spirit is angry with us. Sometimes we forget what they told us, and do wrong, killing one another. Now, we are told you have a good book that tells you all you ought to do; and if we had it and could read it in our tents, maybe we would be better. But we are too old to learn

it now. Teach it to our children,—teach it to
our little ones!" What an answer to prayer!

THE MISSION-HOUSE.

The chapel and the mission-house, which is
the home of the Santee Sioux, were mainly built
by the Indians. A hospital is to be built soon
for them, mainly through the Christian efforts
of William Welsh, Esq., of Philadelphia.

INDIAN LANGUAGE, COUNTING, ETC.

Wah-ge-la, one.
Numpa, two.
Zomina, three.
Do-be, four.
Yap-ta, five.
Sha-ko-pe, six.
Dog, sumka.
Shoko, seven.
Sho-go-lo-ra, eight.
Nim-chalk, nine.
Wieh-grin-ina, ten.
Horse, tu-gon-ka.
Cow or ox, dib-lish.

Candle, pal-a-za-zar.
Cat, how-i-win-go-lar.
Boy, ox-i-la.
Girl, wi-tin-chil-a.
Small, chu-chil-la.
Hat, por-ta.
Snow, of-hene.
Pot or kettle, mushta.
Good, wash-ta.
Don't know, so-lo-wash-
ta.
To-morrow, umpa.

Major Van Voost, at Fort Kearney, always told
the Indians who begged, "Yes, call to-morrow."

So they kept calling, and finally gave him the
name "Umpa."

INDIANS ATTACK LIEUT. W. DOUGHERTY—FIGHT BE-
TWEEN FORTS FETTERMAN AND RENO.

Lieutenant D—— started down from Fort
Reno in the month of March, 1868, and when
within seventeen miles of Reno, he was attacked by a band of Indians while he and his
escort of a sergeant, eight men, four citizens, two
teamsters, and servant, were eating supper at
Camp Dry Fork, on Powder River. The distance between the two posts is ninety-five miles.
Springing to their feet, the soldiers fought off the
Indians till they could harness the teams and
start for Fort Reno. The fight was very severe,
the Indians having every advantage of position,
as they skulk over the bluffs and come in upon
soldiers and others when least expected. By a
bold dash at them, Lieutenant D—— succeeded
in driving them off. They had shot an arrow
into the shoulder of a dog belonging to one of
the soldiers. The dog ran towards Reno, carrying the arrow all the way (seventeen miles), sticking
into the poor creature's hide, causing him immense
pain. And when he came in, his appearance ap-
prised the commanding officer of the condition
Lieutenant D—— and his handful of men were
in, and he at once sent a reinforcement of two

o*   11

companies to rescue the besieged. This was the only way they had of knowing that the party were attacked, and no wonder it was regarded as a providential circumstance.

All reached Fetterman in safety the next evening, and the dog is still a hero among the boys of Company D, 18th United States Infantry.

SPEECH OF "WHITE SHIELD," HEAD CHIEF OF THE ARICKAREES.

Fort Berthold, D. T., July 2d, 1864.

I speak for my brothers, the Arickarees, Gros Ventres, and Mandans. We all live in peace in the same village, as you see us. We have a long time been the friends of the white man, and we will still be. Our grandfathers, the Black Bear of the Arickarees, and the Four Bears of the Gros Ventres, were at the treaty with our white brothers on the Platte a long time ago. They told us to be the friends of our white brothers, and not go to war with our neighbors, the Dakota Sioux, Chippewas, Crees, Assinaboines, Crows, or Blackfeet.

We listened to their words as long as they were heard in council. They have both been killed by the Dakotas; we have none left among us who heard the talk at the treaty on the Platte.

We want a new treaty with our Great Father. We want him to tell us where we must live. We own the country from Heart River to the Black Hills, from there to the Yellowstone River, and north to Moose River.

We are afraid of the Dakotas ; they will kill us, our squaws and children, and steal our horses. We must stay in our village for fear of them. Our Great Father has promised us soldiers to help us keep the Dakotas out of our country. No help has come yet; we must wait. Has our Great Father forgotten his children ? We want to live in our country, or have pay for it, as our Great Father is used to do with his other red children. We, the Arickarees, have been driven from our country on the other side of the Missouri River by the Dakotas. We came to our brothers, the Gros Ventres and Mandans; they received us as brothers, and we all live together in their village. We thank our brothers very much. We want our Father to bring us guns to hunt with, and we want dresses, coats, pants, shirts, and hats for our soldiers, and a different dress for our chiefs. We want a school for our children. Our hearts are good. We do not speak with two tongues. We like to see our white brothers come among us very much. We hear bad talk, but have no ears. When we hear good talk, we have ears.

his

WHITE x SHIELD.

mark

To our Great Father in Washington.

INDIAN TRADING.

A bargain is never concluded so long as anything more can be obtained by an Indian from a
white man. This feature of Indian character is
very old indeed. I remember, when a child, that
when one gave his brother a ball, or anything,
and took it back again, he was called "an Indian
giver." Mr. Hinman gives this experience: "If
an Indian (not a Christian) gives, he expects
soon to ask more in return. This is the selfish
habit of all heathen, and when they have power,
they often accompany their demands for gifts
with threats of killing one's horse, etc., if their
demands are not complied with. They seem to
know nothing of disinterestedness, except among
persons nearly related. An Indian will press you
with his pipe one day, and the next, with a polite
speech about not intending to ask pay for his
pipe, which he treasured highly, intimates that
he needs a blanket !

"One will offer to assist you to work for a day,
and the next ask to borrow two dollars. They
try to get you so indebted to them for favors, that
you cannot decently refuse their requests. In all
their speeches they try to prove to you that you
are indebted to them." So one will ask as few
favors of them as possible. He says, "I was
surprised at the Yankton agency, to have some

young men offer, without any pay, to cut all the timber and do all the work on a building for the council-room for the Mission. The change came sooner under their limited instruction than I had expected, and almost immediately the chief, ' Swan,' offered to cut logs and build a house for a chapel-school at his camp, opposite Fort Randall. The chief, Mad Bull, offered the same for the other end of the reservation, near Choctaw Creek.

" Among those heathens that have borne Christian fruits with the Santees, is 'Little Pheasant,' chief of the wild Brule Sioux, who came down to restore to the Yankton reservation some stolen horses, and promised Paul Mazakuta to take a list of his men desiring instruction. God is moving the hearts of these wild Indians in a wondrous way.

" At our Sunday evening service, over a hundred Yankton warriors and chiefs were present. I preached from the parable of the prodigal son. At the end of this passage, ' Though the elder brother be still jealous of the kindness and mercy shown to you, and thinks your people only fit to go down to the grave with the beasts that perish, yet God is good and just; and though long lost and wandering so many years, now found at last, He will lead you safely to his home.' Dulorio, a chief, said, ' Oh, my friends, this is where we all ought to cry Ko (yes) with a loud voice!'

But the chief, 'Swan,' replied, 'True, true, Koda (friend); but men must not applaud in church. The words they give us ought to be laid up in our hearts.'

"To-day, twenty-two plows are started in the fields, and two in the prairies, to break an additional hundred acres for wheat. A little opposition is shown to dividing the land, but only a few Indians oppose. It is a great step, and one that many are prepared for; but it must be executed by a wise and good man. It is *the death-blow* to heathenism, barbarism, and idleness, and therefore a medicine absolutely necessary to restore health and quicken life; but yet it must be administered by a brave and judicious physician. It is a revolution of habit and of manner of life to the Indian. And in Minnesota, the delay in perfecting it, and the lack of moral support given to those who took farms, caused, as much as anything, the outbreak of 1862, which was, in the beginning, a triumph of the hostile party over the working bands. Philip the deacon, Thomas Whipple, and Alexander Umbeclear, Indian catechists, and two Yankton head soldiers, who volunteered, are on their mission to the wild Sioux. As far as I know, there is a very general desire for schools; and God is surely opening the way for the building up of his kingdom."

RED CLOUD, SPOTTED TAIL, AND THEIR FRIENDS IN
WASHINGTON.

History will point to the visit of these great
chiefs of the Sioux tribes at Washington as the
most important event in their lives, because it
not only staved off a great war threatened on
the plains, but most likely inaugurated a system
of just and fair dealing for the time to come, that
may prevent any more cruel and bloody wars
with the Indians on our frontiers. Hence every
incident that took place there is interesting; and
as it is a costly expense to the government, it is
likely to be discouraged in the future, and if boys
have another chance to see some "big chiefs,"
they will have to go a great way, perhaps to
Nebraska or Dakota, to have a good look at
them.

The party belonging to Zin-tak-gah-lat-skah—
Spotted Tail—left Minnesota before Red Cloud's
from the Powder River country, and arrived first
in Washington; but their interests were the
same, so nothing was done until General Smith
arrived with Red Cloud and reported to the Secretary of War. He then turned them over, as
we say, to the Indian Bureau, which has a suite
of offices, etc. in the Patent Office building in
Washington. The Secretary of the Interior, who
is a member of the cabinet, and General Parker

(Chippewa chief), Indian Commissioner, received them as their charge during their stay in Washington. Before Red Cloud came, however, Spotted Tail had an interview with General Parker. He said:

"The government does not fulfill its treaty promises, and that supplies of goods promised and money owed for lands were not sent to them at the times agreed on, and that the white man, wherever he can find many buffaloes and gold, comes on the Indian's land and takes the Indian's ponies."

Colonel Parker told him of the many difficulties the Indian Bureau had to contend with in order to get moneys through Congress, and the great difficulties such a great government as ours had to go through in conducting all its affairs. But he gave his word to Spotted Tail that all the promises now made in the treaties would be fulfilled, and that they should get the provisions as soon as possible. He said that the Indians must not go to war among themselves, preying on other tribes, nor must they fight any more against the people of the United States, nor steal their cattle or horses.

Spotted Tail said, "He was glad that the Great Father was going to treat them right," but did not commit himself to any policy for the future. He was too good an Indian to make any professions in advance. Spotted Tail has of late years committed no offense except killing Big Mouth in a drunken brawl last winter.

The citizens of Washington have now and then seen Indian delegations at the Capitol. But these lusty fellows, such as Red Cloud, Swift Bear, and others, at once attracted attention.

Their large size and well-developed muscle, tall and graceful in action, especially when speaking in their native eloquence, mark them as objects of surprise and wonder. Their faces were painted in red, yellow, and black stripes. Their ears were pierced, men and women, for large ornaments of silver and bear's teeth. They wore magnificent buffalo robes, ornamented and worked with beads, horse-hair, and porcupine quills. Red Cloud wore red leggins beautifully worked and trimmed with ribbons and beads, and his shirt had as many colors as the rainbow. His robe—made to tell by characters his achievements in battle—was quite rich, and worked with seal-skins. His moccasins pronounced the handsomest ever seen there.

The squaws were ugly, wore short frocks, turned in their toes walking, and had flat or pug-noses.

It was said as a reason for Red Cloud's not bringing his squaws with him, "that Congress-men left their squaws at home!"

Red Cloud said that the pale-faces are more than the grass in numbers. He had come to see

P

the Great Father, and to see if the peace-pipe could not be smoked on the big waters of the Potomac.

The appearance on the balcony of the hotel of the whole party, watching the crowds of pale-faces going to and from the Capitol, created much curiosity, and the Indians remarked to one another that the horse-thieves in the Indian country had a good many brothers in Washington! The negroes were especially attentive, and spoke of them as quite inferior to the colored community. They were assured that Indians never scalp negroes; which is really true, I found, in my interviews with different tribes on the plains. The reason I can only guess at: the curly hair of a negro would not ornament the saddle-bow of an Indian, in the shape of a scalp token of victory.

Meeting at the Bureau.

Long before the Indians came, the passages of the department were filled with a crowd of anxious persons, to inspect the red men as they passed along, and this, besides being unpleasant to them, interfered with their passage into the council-chamber. But soon they all got in, Spotted Tail looking very dignified, with his three companions on one side of the room, while seated in two rows across were Red Cloud and his larger number of chiefs and head-men, and the squaws that came with them.

General John E. Smith, who came with Red Cloud, Colonel Beauvais, of St. Louis, Colonel Bullock, post-trader at Fort Laramie, and others, were present.

After the Indians had got comfortably seated and had passed the pipe around among them a few times, Commissioner Parker, with Secretary Cox, entered the council-room, and were introduced to each Indian of Red Cloud's band, having previously seen Spotted Tail and party. As Indians never speak first, but will sit for hours, Commissioner Parker opened the meeting, saying:

"I am glad to see you to-day. I know that you have come a long way to see your Great Father, the President of the United States. You have had no accident, have arrived here all well, and should be very thankful to the Great Spirit who has kept you safe.

"The Great Father got Red Cloud's message that he wanted to come to Washington and see him, and the President said he might come. We will be ready at any time to hear what Red Cloud has to say for himself and his people, but want him first to hear the Secretary of the Interior, who belongs to the President's council."

The Commissioner stepped aside, and Secretary Cox said:

"When we heard that the chief of the Sioux nation wanted to come to Washington to see the President and the officers of the government, we were glad. We were glad that they themselves said they wanted to come. We know that when people are so far apart as we are from the Sioux, it is very hard to see each other, and to know what each one wants. But when we see each other face to face, we can understand better what is really right, and what we ought to do. The President, General Parker, and myself, and all the officers of the government, want to do what is right." [Here Red Cloud gave a significant look at Spotted Tail across the room.]

"While you are here, therefore, we shall want you to tell us what is in your own hearts, all you feel, and what your condition is, so that we may have a perfect understanding, and that we may make a peace that shall last forever. In coming here, you have seen that this is a very great people, and we are growing all the time. We want to find out the state of things in the Sioux country, so that we may make satisfactory treaties. In a day or two the President will see the chiefs, and in the mean time we want them to get ready to tell him what they have to say, and we will make our answer. We want also to use our influence so that there shall not only be peace between the Indians and whites, but that there shall be no more troubles about difficulties between different bands of Indians."

The Commissioner also said to Spotted Tail that " he thanked him for being present, and was glad of the good will he had for the whites." Most thought the conference was ended, but Red Cloud, through his interpreter, said he had something to say.

Stepping up quickly to the table, and shaking hands with the officials, spoke up in a firm voice, " My friends, I have come a long way to see you and the Great Father, but somehow after I got here, you do not look at me. When I heard the words of the Great Father, allowing me to come, I came right away, and left my women and children. I want you to give them rations, and a load of ammunition to kill game with. I wish you would blow them a message on the wires that I came here safe, all right."

Secretary Cox said he would now only welcome them again, and would telegraph Red Cloud's message, and for the rest, he would see what could be done. To-morrow he would show them what was to be seen about the city. On the next day (Sunday) white people did no business, and on next day evening the President would meet the Indians at the Executive Mansion.

They were invited to have their photographs taken, but Red Cloud declined.

P*

Red Cloud and Spotted Tail went up to the Capitol, where they climbed to the dome, taking a view of the city ; but what most interested them was the large mirrors and the marble busts of two Indian chiefs. They came into the Senate while the Indian Appropriation Bill was under consideration, and while they were fanning themselves incessantly, the interpreter explained what they were doing, but the Indians said nothing. But the greatest event for them was the

Grand Reception to the Indian Delegations by the President, attended by all the Foreign Diplomats.

This took place at the White House on the evening of June 6th. It appeared that the President and Mrs. Grant had arranged with General Parker to give a surprise-party to the Indians, the diplomatic corps, the cabinet, and other dignitaries. What they intended to do was supposed to be a great secret, but it leaked out as early as six o'clock in the afternoon, and many wanted to see the sight.

The carriages of the foreign ministers, secretaries, and attachés of legations were driven up to the entrance of the White House with the ladies and gentlemen of the legation ; then came the members of the cabinet and ladies, and some senators and members of Congress. Soon the Blue, Green and Red Rooms were crowded. The ladies were dressed in their gayest costumes, and the gentlemen had on their Sunday clothes.

About seven o'clock the entire Indian delegation drove up, with Red Cloud, Spotted Tail, with his three braves, in open barouches, and soon shown into the East Room.

This room was brilliantly illuminated, and bouquets of flowers were scattered around.

General Parker welcomed the Indians, and told them they were to see the President and his wife and children, and the members of his great council, the cabinet, and members also of other nations over the big waters to the President, and have a hand-shake, "How" and talk, if they wished. Spotted Tail and braves were seated in the end of the Southeast Room, and Red Cloud and band, with the squaws, along the east side. Spotted Tail and his party were dressed in blue blankets, white leggins, and white shirts, and each had a single eagle's feather stuck in the back of his hair; all their faces had on war-paint, and all the beads and other trinkets they could pile on, adorned their persons.

Red Cloud, in his paint, looked awful, and he wore a head-dress of eagle feathers sewed on red flannel. This was trailed down to his feet, and attracted much notice from its oddity and beauty. Red Dog, his lieutenant and orator, had a beautiful head-gear, as also did several others. It would be impossible to describe the different ornaments worn by these Indians, but they looked as gay as an actor personating Richard the Third on the stage.

The squaws wore short dresses and high bodies or shirts, and their cheeks, noses, and foreheads thickly covered with red paint. Both parties soon set up a lively jabber in Sioux; but General Parker gave a sign, and all were as whist as mice.

The folding-doors were opened from the broad passage-way into the East Room, and soon the President was ushered in with Mrs. Grant, Secretary Fish and wife, Secretary Belknap and wife, Secretary Cox, wife and daughter, Secretary Boutwell and wife, Secretary Robeson and Miss Nellie Grant, Judge Hoar, wife and daughter, Postmaster-General Cresswell, wife and sister, Generals Porter, Dent, Babcock, and others; then followed senators, members, and their wives and other ladies. Next, Minister Thornton, wife and lady friends, with Mr. Secretary Ford, wife, and other attachés of the British legation ; Baron Ge-rolt, wife and daughter, M. and Madame Garcia, and indeed all the representatives of foreign nations on the whole earth but China and Japan. The diplomatic corps did not wear uniforms, but imitated the Indians, who had many insignia of rank in tell-tales of scalps taken, etc., by putting on all their stars and orders, and each wore swal-low-tail coats, white vests, neckties, and gloves and dark pants.

Mrs. Grant was attired in a handsome grena-
dine, and wore a diamond necklace, and japonica
hair adornings. The other ladies seemed to have
vied with each other to out-dress one another,
surpassing even their gay attire at their winter
receptions.

Soon the President with his party had all got
into the East Room, on the west side, the President, with Secretary Fish, General Parker, and
M. Beauvais, the interpreter; next, Mrs. Grant,
Mrs. Parker, and Mrs. Fish, distributed so as to
see all going on, while the Indians lounged lazily
on the sofas staring at their white brethren, both
parties mutually surprised. Then General Parker
made a sign to Spotted Tail with his braves, and
they rose up, one by one, advancing to where
the President and his party were standing, and
the introduction, hand-shaking, etc. began ; the
Indians, as usual, said " How." Red Cloud followed with his band, and all said "How, How,"
shaking hands with each one present. The ladies
seemed to enjoy this very much, laughing and
chatting, and wishing, perhaps, they could speak
the Indian language; for they forgot for a few
moments all the restraints of the situation, and
went in for real fun and frolic with these tawny
sons and daughters of the plains and mountains.

Good rounds of hand-shaking indulged in,
many questions were put and answered through
the interpreters, and a careful examination was

12

made of the hair-dressing, the paint on the
cheeks, the beads, tin ornaments of the Indians,
and the sparkling diamonds of our own people.
The wonder, remarks, and laughter of each party,
as something struck them as singular or ludicrous, were going on all over the room; for the
order was soon broken up, and all mixed in, pale-
faces and Indian alike, quite indiscriminately.

The scene was novel indeed. Here might be
seen the chief of our nation, leaning on his arm
one of the ladies from a foreign court, or a belle
of America mingling in with a group of red-skins,
and trying through an interpreter to converse
with them; the ladies anxious to know the
history of Zin-ta-ga-let-skah, or Stinking-saddle-
cloth, or the Elk-that-bellows-walking, or Man-
afraid-of-his-Horses, etc. Here the bachelor of
the navy was trying to pump an Indian about
his canoes, to please half a dozen pretty girls he
had in tow; but the interpreters being busy, the
Indian could only make signs, give a grunt, a
stare, or grin in reply. Mrs. Grant, with some
ladies, also tried to have a " say" with them on
her own hook, but gave up soon in despair.

Another signal of General Parker, and the
Indians were in their places; next the whites
stood in order, and then the red brethren walked
into the Green, Blue and Red Rooms, and into
the presidential state dining-room.

Here came a new surprise, and a refreshing

sight. The state dining-table was beautifully
decorated with ornaments of gold and silver,
dishes, glasses, flowers, bouquets, etc., and was
fairly loaded down with fruits, berries, ice-cream,
confections, and wines. Side-tables were set out
with delicacies of the season, and it was seen that
the President, with his amiable wife, had gotten
up a strawberry and fruit festival for the wild
men and civilized big bugs of the nations.

In the mean while, the Indians were ranged
round the main table, while the President and
Mrs. Grant and friends proceeded to help the
Indians to all the delicacies they never saw before,
and which they must have regarded as far ahead
of a dog-feast, or the simple wild currants and
plums they pick in the Rocky Mountains.

The ladies of the foreign ministers were not
backward in their assistance. Secretary Boutwell
helped Red Dog to strawberries and cake, Judge
Hoar and Secretary Robeson paid much attention
to the four squaws, cutting cake, and giving them
knick-knacks.

One of the squaws took from the President a
French kiss and a bonbon, and taking her pocket-
book from her bosom, put them both into it, intending to carry it home, three thousand miles,
to her papoose, and then returned it to its hiding-
place, amid roars of laughter, in which President
Grant joined as heartily as anybody.

It was noticed that Red Cloud and Spotted

Tail ate very freely of strawberries, cherries, cakes, bananas, etc., and that while Red Cloud and his party took freely of wine several times, Spotted Tail and his three braves only partook of the " fire-water" once. All then went in and did ample justice to the feast till they were satisfied. If one could imagine a mass of beauty, loveliness, and full dress crowded into rather a small compass, with thirty Indians, and as many more of the male sex of our own color, all eating, chatting, and laughing at the same time, then you have a faint idea of this first great entertainment to a body representing thirty thousand warriors, as a new feature of inaugurating peace for bloodshed, rapine, and murder, in the presidential state dining-room that night.

Then all were marched back into the East Room, seated on sofas, and promenading up, in and down in front of the Indians and their squaws.

Each Indian was presented with a small bouquet by Misses Nellie and Jessie Grant, and a number of their juvenile companions. Spotted Tail, in answer to a question of the President, told him he had eleven children. The President told the interpreter to inform him that he would take one of his boys and educate him, and have him cared for by the government.

Spotted Tail said he would think the matter over.

The President told Red Cloud he would see him in a day or two on business.

The Indians all expressed themselves to the interpreter as having " big hearts," " heap good eat," " like much Great Father," and " much good white squaws."

Mrs. Grant's beautiful gold fan quite took the eyes of the squaws, and they showed much delight, saying they would get some pretty fans for themselves. Soon (as there is an end to all things) the party broke up; the white guests to dream perhaps of some strange play at a theatre, and the Indians to imagine themselves transplanted to the happy hunting-grounds they feel sure they are to enter hereafter, when they have done with hunting the antelope, the deer, and the buffalo, on the plains.

Important Interview.

The Secretary of the Interior, Commissioner Parker, General J. E. Smith, Messrs. Collyer, F. C. Brunot, and the other Indian delegates, met in a grand council at the Patent Office building. All the Indians were dressed in full costume, and seemed to be impressed with the importance of the occasion. Secretary Cox made a long address to the Indians on behalf of the President, assuring them that if they would go to their reservations, and keep the peace, all the rations and goods promised them by the govern-

Q

ment would be sent to them, and agents also, to see that they reached them safely.

In regard to giving them arms and ammunition, he said they would not be given them at present, but after they have kept themselves peaceable on reservations for a time, these would be furnished.

Red Cloud then shook hands with all, and said:

"I came from where the sun sets. You were raised on the chairs. I want to sit where the Indian warrior sat."

Sitting down on the floor, Indian fashion, he went on:

"The Great Spirit has raised me this way. He raised me naked. I make no opposition to the Great Father who sits in the White House. I don't want to fight. I have offered my prayer to the Great Father so that I might come here safe and well. What I have to say to you and to these men, and to my Great Father, is this: Look at me! I was raised where the sun rises, and I came from where he sets. Whose voice was the first heard in this land? The red people's. Who raised the bow? The Great Father may be good and kind, but I can't see it. I am good and kind to white people, and have given my lands, and have now come from where the sun sets to see you. The Great Father has sent his people out there, and left me nothing but an island. Our nation is melting away like the snow on the side of the hills where the sun is warm, while your people are like the blades of grass in the spring when summer is coming. I don't want to see the white people making roads in our country. Now that I have come into my Great Father's land, see if I have any blood when I return home. The white people have sprinkled blood on the blades of grass about the line of Fort Fetterman. Tell the Great Father to remove that fort, and then we will be peaceful, and there will be no more troubles.

" I have yet two mountains in that country,— the Black Hills and Big Horn. I want no roads there. There have been stakes driven in that country, and I want them removed. I have told these things three times, and now have come here to tell them for the fourth time. I have made up my mind to take that way. I don't want my reservation on the Missouri home of these people. I hear that my old men and chil dren are dying off like sheep. The country don't suit them. I was born at the Forks of the Platte. My father and mother told me that the land there belonged to me. From the north and west the red nation has come into the Great Father's house. We are the last of the Ogallallas. We have come to know the facts from our Father, why the promises which have been made to us have not been kept.

" I want two or three traders that we asked for at the mouth of Horse Creek in 1852. There was a treaty made, and the man who made the treaty (alluding to General Mitchell), who performed that service for the government, told the truth. The goods which have been sent out to me have been stolen all along the road, and only a handful would reach to go among my nation.

" Look at me here ! I am poor and naked. I was not provided with arms, and always wanted to be peaceful. The Great Spirit has raised you to read and write, and has put papers before you; but he has not raised me in that way. The men whom the President sends us are soldiers, and all have no sense and no heart. I know it to-day. I didn't ask that the whites should go through my country killing game, and it is the Great Father's fault. You are the people who should keep peace. For the railroads you are passing through my country, I have not received even so much as a brass ring for the land they occupy. [Nor even a shilling an acre for the lands taken from the red men, he might have said.] I wish you to tell my Great Father that the whites make all the ammunition. What is the reason you don't give it to me ? Are you afraid I am going to war ? You are great and powerful, and I am only a handful. I don't want it for that purpose, but to kill game with. I suppose I must in time go to farming, but I can't do it right away."

Secretary Cox promised that their complaints should be attended to by the Great Father.

Another Interview.

The Secretary made a speech, saying that some of the requests made by the Indians concerning their rations and allowing them traders would be acceded to, and that government would do all in its power to make them happy. He announced that they had already received some presents in the shape of blankets, etc., and would receive more in New York on their way home. He repeated what the President said concerning Fort Fetterman. It must remain. They would soon be started on their homeward journey, which information was received by the Indians with unmistakable signs of delight.

Red Cloud spoke in reply, evincing most certainly his dissatisfaction at the determination of the government not to remove Fort Fetterman. He said there was no necessity for its continuance, and its presence was a useless burden and expense to the Great Father. He also took exceptions against the roads running through his country, and intimated that if trouble arose, it would be the. fault of the Great Father.

Red Cloud made another speech, in which he said, " The troops in my country are all fools, and the government is throwing away its money for nothing. The officers there are all whisky-drink-

Q*

ers. The Great Father sends out there the whisky-drinkers because he don't want them around him here. I do not allow my nation or any white man to bring a drop of liquor into my country. If he does, that is the last of him and his liquor. Spotted Tail can drink as much as he pleases on the Missouri River, and they can kill one another if they choose. I do not hold myself responsible for what Spotted Tail does. When you buy anything with my money, I want you to buy me what is useful. I do not want city flour, rotten tobacco, and soldiers' old clothes dyed black, such as you bought for Spotted Tail. I only tell you what is true. You have had a great war, but after it was over you permitted the chiefs who had been fighting to come back."

Secretary Cox explained the treaty of 1868 to the Indians, and said, "The best way is to be friendly and deal honestly with each other. The last treaty made provided for a railroad to be built. The Sioux agreed not to disturb it, and that it should be built. Now, if the road interferes with hunting, we will try to make good the damage by feeding you. We mean that the government shall keep back white men from going into the Indian country, as well as bad Indians from going into the white country. This is what the troops are there for. If any of our people at the forts do not do what is right, the President will punish them and send better men in their places. The same treaty gives the lines of the Indian country."

A map was produced, and the Secretary explained the boundaries fixed in the treaty of 1868. Red Cloud looked on with great interest. He said he was asked to sign the treaty merely to show that he was peaceable, and not to grant their lands. He continued, saying, " This is the first time I have heard of such a treaty, and I do not mean to follow it. I want to know who was the interpreter who interpreted these things to the Indians." The names of three were mentioned, and he said, " I know nothing about it. It was never explained to me."

Bear-in-the-Grass said, " The Great Spirit hears me to-day. I tell nothing but what is true when I say these words of the treaty were not explained. It was only said the treaty was for peace and friendship among the whites. When we took hold of the pen they said they would take the troops away so we could raise children."

Secretary Cox explained that the treaty was signed by more than two hundred different Sioux of all the bands.

Red Cloud—" I do not say the Commissioners lied, but the interpreters were wrong. I never heard a word only what was brought to my camp. When the forts were removed, I came to make peace. You had your war houses. When you removed them, I signed a treaty of peace. We want to straighten things up."

Secretary Cox.—"I have been very careful so that no mistake may be made, and that our words should be as open as daylight, so we may understand what binds the Sioux and ourselves: We are trying to get Congress to carry out our promises, and we want the Indians to do their part. We simply say that this is the agreement made as we remember. We have copies printed. We will give one to Red Cloud so it can be interpreted to him exactly what it is."

Red Cloud said, "All the promises made in the treaty have never been fulfilled. The object of the whites is to crush the Indians down to nothing. The Great Spirit will judge these things hereafter. All the words I sent never reached the Father. They are lost before they get here. I am chief of the thirty-nine nations of Sioux. I will not take the paper with me. It is all lies."

The Secretary distributed copies of the treaty to the interpreting agents and traders present, and adjourned the council till next day, in order that meantime the provisions of the treaty be explained to the Indians.

Final Interview.

They appeared to be much depressed, having reflected over the proceedings of the day before.

They reluctantly came to the meeting next morning, the earnest persuasion of the interpreter,
agent, and traders having induced them to do so.
They stated that their refusal to attend might
result to their injury. The night before Red
Shirt was so much depressed in spirits that he
wanted to commit suicide, saying that he might
as well die here as elsewhere, as they had been
swindled.

Further Explanations.

Commissioner Parker opened the proceedings
by saying the Indians were asked to come up
because it was thought they ought to have something to say before they went home. Secretary Cox said to them he was very sorry to find
out that Red Cloud and his people have not understood what was in the treaty of 1868; therefore he wanted him to come here, so that all
mistakes might be explained and be dismissed.
It was important to know exactly how matters
stood. This government did not want to drive
them. The Secretary then explained, at some
length, the provisions of the treaty, the limits of
the hunting-grounds, the reservation, etc. He
understood that Red Cloud and his band were
unwilling to go on the reservation, but wanted
to live on the head-waters of the Big Cheyenne
River, northeast of Fort Fetterman. This was
outside of the permanent reservation, but inside

the part reserved for hunting-ground. The Secretary was willing to say, if that would please
them, he would make it so, and have their business agents there; this would still keep white
people off the hunting-ground. The government
would give them cattle and food and clothing, so
as to make them happy in their new home. The
Secretary said he would write down the names of
the men in whom the Indians have confidence,
and want for their agent and traders. He desired
to find out whether they were good men, and
could be trusted by the government. He was
sorry the Indians felt bad on finding out what
was in the treaty; but the best way was to tell it
all, so there might not be any misunderstanding.

Red Cloud, having shaken hands with the Secretary and Commissioner Parker, seated himself
on the floor, and said:

"What I said to the Great Father, the President, is now in my mind. I have only a few
words to add this morning. I have become tired
of speaking. Yesterday, when I saw the treaty,
and all the false things in it, I was mad. I suppose it made you the same. The Secretary explained it this morning, and now I am pleased.
As to the goods you talked about, I want what
is due and belongs to me. The red people were
raised with the bow and arrow, and are all of one
nation; but the whites, who are educated and
civilized, swindle me; and I am not hard to

swindle, because I cannot read and write. We have thirty-two nations (or bands), and have a council-house the same as you have. We held a council before we came here, and the demands I have made upon you from the chiefs I left behind me are all alike. You whites have a chief you go by, but all the chief I go by is God Almighty. When he tells me anything that is for the best, I always go by his guidance. The whites think the Great Spirit has nothing to do with us, but he has. After fooling with us and taking away our property, they will have to suffer for it hereafter. The Great Spirit is now looking at us, and we offer him our prayers.

"When we had a talk at the mouth of Horse Creek, in 1852, you made a chief of Conquering Bear and then destroyed him, and since then we have had no chief. You white people did the same to your great chief. You killed one of our great fathers. The Great Spirit makes us suffer for our wrong-doing. You promised us many things, but you never performed them. You take away everything. Even if you live forty years or fifty years in this world and then die, you cannot take all your goods with you. The Great Spirit will not make me suffer, because I am ignorant. He will put me in a place where I will be better off than in this world. The Great Spirit raised me naked and gave me no arms. Look at me. This is the way I was raised. White

men say we are bad, we are murderers, but I
cannot see it." [Red Cloud did not use this slang
phrase,—no Indian speaks so,—and the interpreters spoil much of the beauty of idiom in
translating what the Indian says. He meant,
" I did not so understand it."]

" We gave up our lands whenever the whites
came into our country. Tell the Great Father I
am poor. In earlier years, when I had plenty of
game, I could make a living; I gave land away,
but I am too poor for that now. I want something for my land. I want to receive some pay
for the lands where you have made railroads.
My Father has a great many children out West
with no ears, brains, or heart. You have the
names to the treaty of persons professing to be
chiefs, but I am chief of that nation. Look at
me. My hair is straight. I was free born on
this land. ⌐ An interpreter who signed the treaty
has curly hair. He is no man. I will see him
hereafter. I know I have been wronged. The
words of my Great Father never reach me, and
mine never reach him. There are too many
streams between us. The Great Spirit has raised
me on wild game. I know he has left enough
to support my children for awhile. You have
stolen Denver from me. You never gave me
anything for it. Some of our people went there
to engage in farming, and you sent your white
children and scattered them all away. Now I

have only two mounds left, and I want them for myself and people. There is treasure in them. You have stolen mounds containing gold. I have for many years lived with the men I want for my superintendent, agent, and traders, and am well acquainted with them. I know they are men of justice; they do what is right. If you appoint them, and any blame comes, it will not be on you, but on me. I would be willing to let you go upon our land when the time comes; but that would not be until after the game is gone. I do not ask my Great Father to give me anything. I came naked, and will go away naked. I want you to tell my Great Father I have no further business. I want you to put me on a straight line. I want to stop in St. Louis to see Robert Campbell, an old friend." Red Cloud then pointed to a lady in the room, saying, "Look at that woman. She was captured by Silver Horn's party. I wish you to pay her what her captors owe her. I am a man true to what I say, and want to keep my promise. The Indians robbed that lady there, and through your influence I want her to be paid."

Secretary Cox replied to Red Cloud that the treaty showed how the land was to be paid for. They were to be given cattle, agricultural instruments, seeds, houses, blacksmith-shops, teachers, etc., and food and clothing. The land is good in two ways: one is to let the game grow for the hunt; the other, to plow it up and get corn and wheat, and other things out of it, and raise cattle on it. The reason why so many white men live on their land is that they treat it in this way. He would correct Red Cloud in a remark made by him. " The whites do not expect to take their goods with them into the other world. We know as well as the Indians do that we go out of the world as naked as when we came into it; but while here in the world we take pleasure in build-ing great houses and towns, and make good bread to eat.

" We are trying to teach them to do the same things, so that they may be as well off as we are. Here [pointing to Commissioner Parker] is the Commissioner of Indian Affairs, who is a chief among us. He belonged to a race who lived there long before the white man came to this country. He now has power, and white people obey him, and he directs what shall be done in very important business. We will be brethren to you in the same way if you follow his good example and learn our civilization."

Red Cloud responded, " I don't blame him for being a chief. He ought to be one. We are all of one nation."

Secretary Cox.—" Those Indians who become chiefs among us do so by learning the white man's customs, and ceasing to be dependent as children. I was glad to hear Red Cloud say he would not go away angry. General Smith will see that you get good presents. But these are small things compared with the arrangements that will be made to make you prosperous and happy. Some of the Peace Commissioners will go to your country to see that you are well treated. I do not want you to think the days coming are black days. I want you to think they will be bright and happy days. Be of good spirit. If you feel like a man who is lost in the woods, we will guide you out of them to a pleasant place. You will go home two days from now. One day will be spent by General Smith in New York to get you the presents."

Red Cloud replied, " I do not want to go that way. I want a straight line. I have seen enough of towns. There are plenty of stores between here and my home, and there is no occasion to go out of the way to buy goods. I have no business in New York. I want to go back the way I came. The whites are the same everywhere. I see them every day. As to the improvement of the red men, I want to send them here delegates to Congress."

Secretary Cox said he would be guided by General Smith as to the route homeward. He was not particularly anxious the Indians should go to New York. This ended the interview. The Indians shook hands with the Secretary and Commissioner Parker, and then hurried from the room, followed by the crowd of persons who had gathered at the door.

Little Swan's Speech.

Little Swan, a Sioux chief, said to the President about the Indian situation :

" What my Great Father asks for, peace, is all very well. If I had my own way, it would be all right, and there would be no more fighting; but I saw in the Congress, when I went there, on Thursday, that all the big chiefs there did not agree very well. It is the same with my young men. They are not all of one mind; but I will do my best to make them of one mind, and to keep the peace. I am a bad young man, too, and have made much trouble. I did not get to be a big chief by good conduct, but because I was a great fighter, like you, my Great Father."

These words were really delivered. The allusion to Congress and to the President hit the nail on the head ; at least, it is thought so.

Spotted Tail in New York.

On the 14th of June, the four lords of the desert, Spotted Tail, Swift Bear, Fast Bear, and Yellow Hair, had a busy day. They began in the morning with a visit to the French frigate,

Magicienne, where they were received by Admiral Lefeber and his staff, and a salute was fired in their honor. They were conducted to the admiral's state-room and regaled upon cakes and champagne. The latter they enjoyed immensely, but Captain Poole wisely limited them to one glass each, not desiring to witness a scalping scene on his frigate. After this repast, the red men were conducted all over the ship. The admiral then had one of the fifteen-inch guns loaded with powder, and each one of the Indians pulled the lanyard in turn. This was royal sport for the Indians, and as each gun was fired they looked eagerly for the splash of the ball which they thought was in the cannon. It was impossible to explain to them that the gun was loaded with powder only, as when they visited the Brooklyn navy-yard a shotted gun was fired for their especial edification, and their delight was then to watch for the ball striking the water.

After the visit to the frigate, the Indians returned to the Astor House, where a crowd of five or six hundred people was assembled. The private entrance on Vesey Street was besieged by an excited multitude anxious to get a peep at the "red-skins," but they were disappointed, as the stage drove up to the Barclay Street entrance.

Although they had been to a certain extent amused by what they have seen in New York, still, they were all anxious to get back home.

R*

Captain Poole says that the crowds which dogged their footsteps wherever they went annoyed them considerably, and it is owing to this that they have departed so abruptly. Many invitations were sent them, including one from James Fisk, Jr., to visit his steamers, and one from the officers of the turret ship Miantonomah. Spotted Tail, however, declined to accept either, being tired of Eastern life. He also refused to take a trip up the Hudson, saying that he and his brethren all wanted to go home.

Before the Indians' departure from Washington, President Grant handed four hundred dollars to Captain Poole, and directed that each chief should choose presents to the value of one hundred dollars. They were accordingly taken to an up-town store, where each filled a large trunk with articles of various kinds. Combs, brushes, umbrellas, blankets, and beads seemed particularly to please their fancy. Swift Bear wanted to take about a dozen umbrellas, but was dissuaded from it by Captain Poole.

They took a Pacific Railroad car on the Hudson River Railroad, at eight o'clock in the evening.

Red Cloud in New York.

Red Cloud changed his mind, and came on to New York to attend a great meeting of friends of the red men, at Cooper Institute. On the evening of June 16th, the party were treated to a grand reception, at which it was supposed that no less than five thousand were present. Among other things, Red Cloud said :

"I have tried to get from my Great Father what is right and just. I have not altogether succeeded. I want you to believe with me, to know with me, that which is right and just. I represent the whole Sioux nation. They will be grieved by what I represent. I am no Spotted Tail, who will say one thing one day, and be bought for a fish the next. Look at me ! I am poor, naked, but I am chief of a nation. We do not ask for riches; we do not want much; but we want our children properly trained and brought up. We look to you for that. Riches here do no good. We cannot take them away with us out of this world, but we want to have love and peace. The money, the riches, that we have in this world, as Secretary Cox lately told me, we cannot take these into the next world. If this is so, I would like to know why the Commissioners who are sent out there do nothing but rob to get the riches of this world away from us. I was brought up among traders and those who came out there in the early times. I had good times with them; they treated me mostly always right; always well; they taught me to use clothes, to use tobacco, to use fire-arms and ammunition. This was all very well until the Great

Father sent another kind of men out there,—men who drank whisky ; men who were so bad that the Great Father could not keep them at home, so he sent them out there."

Reception of Red Cloud at Home.

Doubtless speculators and contractors were disappointed when they heard, on General Smith's return, of Red Cloud's satisfaction, and what he said about being peaceable, and using his influence among his warriors. A thousand lodges were gathered to receive him, and the demonstrations made over his return exceeded any the oldest Indian had ever seen before.

On the way out, Red Cloud gave General Smith his reason for asking the government for the seventeen horses. He did not really need them, but made up his mind that if he had been sent back on foot from Pine Bluff, or Fort Laramie, his tribes might think he was lightly esteemed by our authorities, and thereupon they might begin to despise him. His influence would decrease, and he might be unsuccessful in preventing war. He merely wished to accept of them as a tribute to his exalted position as a great warrior among his people. The general said that his appearance, with his whole party well mounted, had the desired effect, and Red

Cloud's warriors saw at a glance that the chief was believed to be a great warrior by the Great Father at Washington.

CONCLUSION.

Boys love fair play, and I know they will make every allowance for the poor Indian, who is, in his wild state, indeed a savage, born and bred up among the wild beasts of the forest; untutored and cruel to his enemies, whether man or beast. We must take him as we find him, then, and not as some sensation writers would make us believe, to be *more noble and generous* than many white men. For we may find many noble examples of generosity among them, in freeing captives and forgiving wrongs done to them; but they have been for over two hundred years victims of the white man's dishonest dealings, and I think that we would do pretty much as the Indian does, if we were Indians, and had been taught the lesson of our forefathers' wrongs. The Indian agents have been in former years mostly dishonest, and cheated those they should have remembered were simple children of the forest; and though they were knowing enough to perceive they were badly dealt with and did not get their due, could not tell just where the cheating came in. You remember the story of a white man and an Indian going a hunting on shares. Well, they killed a wild turkey and a buzzard, the latter good for naught. They sat down on a log to divide the game. " Now," said the white man, " You take the buzzard, and I'll take the turkey; or, I'll take the turkey, and you take the buzzard." The Indian opened his eyes wide, and replied, " Seems to me you talk all buzzard to me, and no talk turkey."

Very little " talk turkey" has the Indian experienced in dealing with the whites. Indeed, you can judge of fair dealing, or want of it, when it is known that an agent came out our way to pay off annuities with blankets, etc. These were " shoddy blankets," and when one tribe was paid off with them, the agent bought them all back again with bad whisky, and went on farther, to pay off other tribes in like manner.

So one agent carried out to California some annuity goods to pay off Indians, according to treaty, *and among them were several thousand elastics ; and yet no Indian wears a stocking!*

The bad Indians *must be punished, just as bad boys, who do wrong; and the army alone can deal with refractory Indians, whose tender mercies are most cruel to white men, women, and children.*

General Sherman came out here in 1868 as one of " the Peace Commission," to personally investigate the whole matter. On his arrival at Cheyenne and at Denver, a large number of pioneers were ready to insult him, because he would not

make a speech, and authorize them to band together and kill Indians wherever found !*

This idol of the American people they were
not willing to trust to do justice to both parties,
after visiting among the tribes on the plains,
and in New Mexico, and seen things for himself. Such is human nature. But the general
could wait his time, and the judgment of the
whole people will be, to give him credit for a far-
sighted policy, the result of a wise head and an
understanding heart, that swerves neither to the
right hand nor the left, so it be in the plain path
of duty ! Why not believe and trust him in the
future, as we have in the past ? We are to
take care how we draw down upon our nation
God's anger for *previous* years of injustice and
bad treatment; and if General Grant had done
nothing more to signalize his administration than
the appointment of honest agents to look after
the welfare of Indians on reservations, while leaving to Generals Sherman and Sheridan the dealing with wild, refractory bands of pagan savages,
roaming over the settlements on the plains, to do
their murderous work of brutalities that sicken
the heart to contemplate, and make to the suf-

* A man whom I had some respect for, said to me at this
time, " If we can get up a smart Indian war now, wouldn't it
be the making of Cheyenne?" He had an eye to an army
contract. General Sherman would probably have called him
a " bummer."

ferers a welcome death as speedily as possible,—
he would be one of the greatest Presidents we
have had.

I have thus tried to give an impartial history
of the "Indian Question," showing the characteristics of our white settlers in their treatment of
the Indians; and, on the other hand, painting
the savage as he is, in his wild, cruel nature, and
with whom we have to deal with all the wisdom
our government can devise. I have done so
with a purpose. This is to show how little
Christianity has done thus far to make white
men just, fair, and honorable, and to gain the
respect of the red man for the Christian's God.
It is a sad reflection, too, that we are doing so
little, and that the world's conversion is so far,
so very far away in the future. *There is a dread-
ful responsibility resting somewhere!*

If our religion is not a sham, we must meet
the question as it has never been met before.
Infidelity has no surer or more deadly weapon
than that which it wields to-day against our professions of love for the souls of our fellow-men,
while we content ourselves with expressions only
of that love. It is hollow, superficial, and full
of cant. If our religion does not take a deeper
form, and go out in active sympathy and work,
it will surely perish, and deserves to perish.
Men ask for results, and it is right they should.
The tree is known by its fruits. We cannot

gather grapes of thorns, or figs of thistles. This is Christ's standard. Do we belong to Him, or are we false, hypocritical children of the Evil One?

Our Saviour said, " It must needs be that offences come; but woe to that man by whom the offence cometh!" Now, if so be that God, who is just, shall require that we atone for all the wrongs perpetrated upon the red men ever since the Mayflower landed her pilgrims on the shores of New England (for there is no repentance for nations at the day of judgment), or that our children shall suffer in some way for it,—who shall say it is not a righteous retribution? "Vengeance is mine, I will repay, saith the Lord."

LORD'S PRAYER IN SIOUX LANGUAGE.

Ate-un-yan-pi, Mar-pi-ya, ekta, nan-ke-cin, Ni-caje, wa-kan-da-pi, kta, Ni-to-ki-con-ze, ukte, Mar-pi-ya, ekta, ni-taw-a-cin, econ-pi, kin, nun-we ; au-pe-tu, kin, de, au-pe-tu, iyoki, aguyapi, kin, un-ju, miye.

Qu, un-kix, una, e-ciux-in-yan, ecaun-ki, con-pi, nicun-ki-ci-ca-ju-ju-pi; he, iye-cen, wau-ur-tan-ipi, kui, un-ki-ci-ca-ju-ju, miye. Qa, taku, wani-yu-tan, kin, en, unkayapa, xui, pa, Tuka, taku, vice, cin, etanhan, eunt-da-ku-pi. Wo-ki-con-ze-kin, no-wax-a ki, kin, ga, wouitan, kin, hena-kiy, a, ouihanke, wanin, nitawa, heon. Amen.

s

The name of God is Wakantanka. The name of the Lord is Itankan.

APOSTLES' CREED.

Wakantanka iyotan Waxaka Atezapikin parpia, maka iyahna kage cin, he wicawada:

Qua Jesus Christ Itankan unyapi, he Cinhintku hece un Mary eciyapi kin, utanhan toupi; Pontius Pilate kakixya, Canicipauega, en okantanpi, te qua rapi; Wanagi yakonpi etka I, Iyamnican ake kini; Wankan marpiya ekta iyaye. Qua Wakantanka, ateyapi iyotan waxaka yanke cin, etapa kin eciy atanhan iyotanka; Heciyatankan meaxta nipi, qua tapi kin, hena yuuytaya nicayaco u kta, Woniya Wakan kin he wicauada; Omniciza, wakan Owaneaya kin Owaneaya kin, Wicaxta Wakan Okodakiciye kin; Woartani kajujupi kin; Wicatancan kini kte cin; Qua wicociououihanke wanin ce cin; Hena ouasin wieawada. Amen.

DISTANCES.

From Omaha to Cheyenne is five hundred and sixteen miles; Cheyenne to Greeley, on Cache-la-poudre River, fifty-four miles; Cheyenne to Denver, one hundred and eleven miles; same to Golden City; Cheyenne to Sherman, thirty-three miles (this is eight thousand two hundred and forty-two feet above the level of the sea); to

Fort Sanders, fifty-four miles; Laramie City, fifty-six miles; Salt Lake, five hundred and thirty-five miles; Salt Lake to Lake's Crossing, Truckee River, four hundred and ninety-nine miles; Truckee to Sacramento, one hundred and nineteen miles; thence to San Francisco, one hundred and twenty-four miles; Omaha to San Francisco, one thousand seven hundred and ninety-two miles.

Cheyenne, northwest to Fort Fetterman, one hundred and seventy miles; Fort Reno (abandoned), two hundred and seventy-four miles; Fort Phil. Kearney (abandoned), three hundred and thirty-nine miles; Fort C. F. Smith, four hundred and twenty-nine miles; Helena, Montana, six hundred and nine miles; Junction of Bear River to City of Rocks, one hundred and eighty-one miles; to Boïsé City, three hundred and ninety-three miles; to Idaho City, four hundred and forty miles; to Owyhee, four hundred and seventy-five miles; to Fort Ellis, Montana, six hundred miles; to Fort Brown, Sweetwater, four hundred and forty-two miles.

THE END.